Allen Carr

Your Personal **STOP SMOKING PLAN**

Allen Carr

Your Personal STOP SMOKING PLAN

ARCTURUS

To Sue Bolshaw, Colleen Dwyer, Cris Hay, Sam Carroll, Jenny
Rutherford and Jennie Gillian in recognition of their significant
and meaningful contributions to Allen Carr's Easyway organization.
You are superstars of Easyway.

Thanks also to Tim Glynne-Jones and Nigel Matheson for editorial
input in the creation of this dynamic new kind of Allen Carr book.

ARCTURUS

This edition published in 2015 by Arcturus Publishing Limited
26/27 Bickels Yard, 151–153 Bermondsey Street,
London SE1 3HA

ISBN: 978-1-78404-501-2
AD004326UK

Printed in China

Contents

Foreword

By John Dicey, Worldwide Managing Director & Senior Therapist, Allen Carr's Easyway

For a third of a century Allen Carr chain-smoked 60 to 100 cigarettes a day. With the exception of acupuncture, he'd tried pretty much all the conventional methods to quit without success. Eventually he gave up even trying to stop, believing "once a smoker always a smoker". Then he discovered something which motivated him to try again:

"I went overnight from a hundred cigarettes a day to zero – without any bad temper or sense of loss, void or depression. On the contrary, I actually enjoyed the process. I knew I was already a non-smoker even before I had extinguished my final cigarette and I've never had the slightest urge to smoke since."

It didn't take Allen long to realize that he had discovered a method that would enable any smoker to quit:

- EASILY, IMMEDIATELY AND PERMANENTLY

- WITHOUT USING WILLPOWER, AIDS, SUBSTITUTES OR GIMMICKS

- WITHOUT SUFFERING DEPRESSION OR WITHDRAWAL SYMPTOMS

- WITHOUT GAINING WEIGHT

After using his smoking friends and relatives as guinea pigs, he gave up his lucrative profession as a qualified accountant and set up a clinic to help other smokers to quit. He called his method "EASYWAY" and so successful has it become that there are now Allen Carr's Easyway clinics in more than 150 cities in 50 countries worldwide. Best-selling books based on his method are now translated into over 38 languages, with more being added each year.

Allen Carr was invited to speak at the 10th World Conference on Tobacco

& Health held in Beijing in 1998, an honour that the most eminent physician would be proud of. His method and reputation could receive no higher commendation in that he was the first non-medically trained expert to receive such an invitation. Allen Carr's Easyway organization is now widely accepted as the world's leading authority on stopping smoking and the method has been successfully applied to alcohol, weight issues, fear of flying, gambling, debt and a whole host of legal and illegal drugs.

I'm aware that the claims of the method's success might appear far-fetched or exaggerated, at times even outrageous. That was certainly my reaction when I first heard them. I was incredibly fortunate to attend Allen's clinic in London in 1997, yet I did so under duress. I had agreed to go, at the request of my wife, on the understanding that when I walked out of the clinic and remained a smoker she would leave it at least 12 months before hassling me about stopping smoking again. No one was more surprised than me, or perhaps my wife, that Allen Carr's Easyway method set me free from my 80-a-day addiction.

I was so inspired that I badgered Allen Carr and Robin Hayley (now Chairman of Allen Carr's Easyway) to let me get involved in their quest to cure the world of smoking. I was incredibly fortunate to have succeeded in convincing them to allow me to do so. Being trained by Allen Carr was one of the most rewarding experiences of my life. To be able to count Allen as not only my coach and mentor but also my friend was an amazing honour and privilege. Allen Carr and Robin Hayley trained me well – I went on personally to treat more than 30,000 smokers at Allen's original London clinic, and am part of the team that have taken Allen's method from Berlin to Bogota, from New Zealand to New York, from Sydney to Santiago. Tasked by Allen to ensure that his legacy achieves its full potential, we've taken Allen Carr's Easyway from videos to DVD, from clinics to apps, from computer games to audio books, to online programmes and beyond. We've a long way to go and this book will play a huge part in our quest.

The honour of adding a light editorial touch to update and develop Allen's method in this book has fallen to me. This enables us to look at issues such as e-cigarettes that have emerged in recent years and, in fact, look at all uses of all forms of nicotine. Please bear with me as you read this short but important foreword – believe me, it's important to do so whether you're a user of e-cigarettes and other nicotine products or not. I promise to leave you in Allen Carr's safe hands after that.

E-cigarettes and all that!

Whether you're a cigarette, cigar, or pipe smoker, or a vaper (user of e-cigarettes), nicotine patch wearer, nicotine gum chewer, nicotine inhalator, snus, or dip user – in fact a user of nicotine via any delivery device available – THIS BOOK WILL SET YOU FREE.

If you've never vaped or used other nicotine devices you might make the mistake of thinking this section of the book simply doesn't apply to you. Don't! The rest of this book will enable you to find it ridiculously easy to stop smoking – you'll never have to suffer with nicotine addiction again. But to avoid falling back into the nicotine trap in the future you must understand it completely.

You're escaping from the torture of nicotine addiction, not just escaping from smoking. If you harbour thoughts that perhaps in the future you might try an e-cigarette just to see what it's like, you'll be susceptible to falling back into the trap. This is particularly important as e-cigarettes in particular are being marketed ruthlessly across all media. One of the most powerful and influential marketing machines on the planet is ramping up its activities once again. Their target? You and your kids! One puff of a cigarette, cigar, pipe, "joint" with tobacco, or intake of nicotine by any means will trap you again. Understand why you need to avoid all nicotine and you will not only be set free forever, but find it ridiculously easy to stop and, more importantly, stay stopped.

OK, so let's understand how e-cigarettes came to be supported by much of the anti-tobacco establishment (people such as Action on Smoking and Health in the UK).

"Safer nicotine delivery systems" – such as e-cigarettes – were first supported by those in the medical and scientific establishment who realized, in the late 1990s and early 2000s, that nicotine replacement therapy (NRT) based programmes were failing to significantly reduce smoking rates. Ironically, some of these individuals were those responsible for the conception and implementation of those failing NRT-based programmes and policies.

Having failed with the policy of using nicotine to cure addiction to nicotine, they concluded that the real problem was that nicotine addicts were simply not getting large enough or frequent enough doses of nicotine from NRT and that delivery mechanisms such as nicotine patches and nicotine gum weren't efficient or effective enough at delivering the drug.

The creation of a harm reduction strategy for smokers was therefore born entirely from the tobacco control establishment's spectacular failure to help smokers to stop smoking with NRT programmes and products they themselves supported and devised over two decades. Usefully for the pharmaceutical industry, and others with vested interests, harm reduction doesn't necessarily involve the awkward task of getting the addict to stop taking the drug.

The fact is, the idea of using safer electronic nicotine delivery systems to deliver nicotine in a cleaner and possibly less harmful way seemed appealing to many. If permanently converting smokers of normal cigarettes to less harmful e-cigarettes could be achieved, it was thought that tens of millions of lives could be saved.

But even if the harm reduction idea HAD worked, Allen Carr's Easyway method would still have had a hugely important part to play in setting people free of nicotine addiction. Those who might become solely addicted to e-cigarettes would still suffer from a number of serious negative factors affecting them and their families.

Who gains from nicotine addiction?

In 2014 research commissioned by Action on Smoking and Health indicated that the cost to the National Health Service caused by smoking was £2bn ($3bn) a year with the cost of social care for older smokers around £1.1bn ($1.6bn) a year. UK tax revenue from tobacco excise and VAT in 2013 was £12.3 billion ($18bn)!

You don't have to be an accountant to work out that the benefit to the Treasury of continued smoking and nicotine addiction is more than £9 billion ($13.5bn) per year. Since 1990 the annual UK tax revenue from tobacco has doubled. It is destined to always go only in one direction. That's up!

Business wins – governments lose

Can you think of a reason why on one hand, international global corporations such as Microsoft, Vodafone, IBM, Ford, Total, Esso, Pfizer, and BMW, to name but a few, regularly contract the services of Allen Carr's Easyway to help their employees stop smoking, yet the government, Department of Health, and the National Health Service do not?

In the world of commerce it's universally accepted that an employee who smokes will cost their employer in excess of £2,000 a year ($3,000) in lost productivity and increased absenteeism because of sickness.

That fact alone makes acquiring our services compelling in terms of return on investment for our corporate clients, let alone the advantages of having a happier and healthier workforce. We even offer our corporate clients the same money-back guarantee that we offer our private clients. If their employee doesn't quit by the time they complete the programme, we refund the fee for that employee.

In short – these companies save a fortune by helping their employees to stop smoking.

The growing number of health insurance companies around the world who pay for their policyholders to attend our clinics also save a fortune when they contract our services. The cost of maintaining their policyholders' good health is dramatically reduced when they stop smoking – as are the former smokers' premiums.

However, a nicotine addict that frees themself from their addiction costs the Treasury money in reduced tax revenues for their lifetime. It's the complete opposite of the effect when a company employee or insurance policyholder escapes from their addiction.

Can you see how governments might be financially disincentivized to help smokers, vapers, or any kind of nicotine addict escape? Of course, none of the sums quoted take into account the fact that smokers die many years before their time, thus easing the burden on pension budgets.

Early on in the development of the e-cigarette market, manufacturers assured the tobacco control community and other interested parties that the target market for e-cigarettes was existing smokers and that the marketing positioning and messaging for the e-cigarette would be as a quit smoking aid.

That isn't quite how it has turned out. By 2014 there were still no controls over who could sell them, who could buy them, what was in them, and how the product might be advertised. It's back to the days of *Mad Men*, using sex to sell slavery and addiction. In fact, 2014 saw the first UK TV advert showing smoker-like behaviour in decades – an attractive, alluring model exhaling smoke-like vapour. The brands using these tactics are clearly targeting everyone, not just smokers. The advertising creatives on Madison Avenue can once again use humour, sex and hugely aspirational imagery to sell nicotine addiction!

Of course these ads are aimed primarily at young people, as are the packaging, flavours and pack designs. E-cigarettes have been marketed aggressively to children. The statistics show that increasing numbers of children are being drawn into using them as well, with a 2014 study being the first to confirm that more kids are using e-cigarettes at a younger age than would use normal cigarettes, and that more of those kids will eventually smoke real cigarettes. The nicotine industry of course loves this. Get the addicts younger and you maximize the lifetime income per user. One can only assume that the Treasury department feels likewise.

A certain number of kids have always tried out cigarettes, but the way e-cigarettes are creeping into everyday life is different. It's creating a new gateway into smoking and nicotine addiction.

Because zero nicotine capsules or liquid can be purchased, youngsters really can say that the e-cigarette they are using is not addictive. Who's to know different? Especially when they come in flavours such as bubble-gum, watermelon, cotton candy, popcorn, and cherry cheesecake. Who do you think those flavours are targeting? Your kids!

Of course before too long the zero-nicotine capsules are discarded in favour of the ones that contain nicotine.

As if getting children as young as 12 addicted to nicotine isn't bad enough, we've warned for years that e-cigarettes will prove to be a gateway into "smoking for real" for most of those youngsters. The latest studies confirm our worst fears.

You can imagine how the kids get sucked in. Firstly, the peer pressure to move on to "the real thing" exists already, but more significantly for the simple reason that no e-cigarette will ever deliver nicotine as efficiently as a cigarette. All addicts eventually end up looking for ways to get more of their drug into their bloodstream faster, so it is with nicotine. That's where cigarettes come in.

All this means that things are not going quite as the architects of tobacco harm reduction policy might have wished. But again, there are those who would argue that, in spite of the points I've made, if the payback of such a policy was the saving of tens of millions of lives, it might be worth it.

Therefore the big question that remains is: are e-cigarettes helping smokers to stop smoking?

In February 2014 Allen Carr's Easyway organization tasked a research company to survey over 1,000 adult e-cigarette users in the UK. The objective was to establish their attitude towards e-cigarettes and smoking.

The results were based on smoker and e-cigarette user patterns amongst people who had used e-cigarettes in the UK since 1 January 2014.

The survey indicated that 84 per cent of e-cigarette users regularly continue to smoke cigarettes as well as e-cigarettes. And this is where the harm reduction policy falls down. If smokers continue to smoke – even a handful of cigarettes a day – the harm reduction model that saves millions of lives simply doesn't work.

Now, if you're one of the few e-cigarette or other nicotine product users who have successfully stopped smoking but remain hooked on nicotine, you're very much the exception. For you the advantages of becoming entirely free from nicotine remain compelling – after all, isn't that why you're reading this book? So please, don't be offended by our assertion that the vast majority of e-cigarette users continue to smoke; it happens to be true. While you continue to remain addicted to nicotine, you remain vulnerable to smoking and all the downsides of addiction. Getting free from those is priceless.

A new generation of nicotine addicts has been recruited via the e-cigarette phenomenon. Equally devastating is the fact that smokers who previously might have abstained from smoking at times when they were not able to smoke, for example at home, or in the car with kids, at non-smoker friends' houses, will now vape. This means they're actually consuming more nicotine than they might have done before the introduction of e-cigarettes; they smoke when they can and vape when they can't.

In addition to that, how many former smokers who quit with willpower are being sucked back into nicotine addiction by unbridled e-cigarette availability, marketing, and advertising?

What does it all mean?

In summary then, we have a new generation of nicotine addicts in development. Existing smokers are likely to be increasing their intake of nicotine rather than decreasing it (by smoking AND vaping); there continues to be a re-normalization of smoker/smoker-like behaviour; many former smokers are being drawn back into nicotine addiction and smoking; little is known of the health effects of long-term nicotine use in the dual form of smoking and vaping (or just vaping for that matter); and those with a vested interest in "The Nicotine Industry" will lead the field in establishing how harmful or otherwise it may be (and we all know how well that's turned out in the past).

This is an industry with a proven track record of fraud on a global scale, built on lies, bribery, corruption, suppression of study data that's resulted in millions of lives being lost, direct involvement in organized international tobacco smuggling, aggressive marketing to children in the developing world, as well as more covert targeting of youngsters in other parts of the world where direct marketing to children is forbidden. This is the most powerful industry on the planet and it saddens me to admit, they ARE winning "The Nicotine War".

Neither you nor your kids want to be a casualty or victim of that war; that's why you're reading this book. As Allen Carr guides you through his amazing method over the coming chapters, he talks exclusively about cigarettes. In doing so he's referring to nicotine in all its forms.

Carry on smoking, vaping, or smoking AND vaping, as you read the book; don't be tempted to cut down or control your intake as you read. If you haven't smoked a cigarette for a long period, there's no need for you to do so – at the end of the book when you're asked to have a final cigarette or e-cigarette just confirm in your mind that you've already done so. In the unlikely event that you've vaped without smoking for a long period – just carry on vaping as you read – you'll still be able to relate virtually all of the text to your vaping. Please make sure that you do that as you read. The same goes for you if you are using patches, gum, snus, dip, or nicotine in any form. When it comes to the final cigarette at the end of the book, just have one final e-cigarette or shot of nicotine in whatever form you've been using it.

This is the most up-to-date, cutting-edge version of Allen Carr's Easyway method in print to date. Follow Allen Carr's instructions and you'll find it not only easy to be free, but you'll actually enjoy the whole process of quitting.

That might sound too good to be true at the moment, but read on. You've got nothing to lose and absolutely everything to gain. Let me pass you into the safest of hands – OVER TO ALLEN CARR.

• Notes boxes are scattered throughout the text. Please use these to make notes about any points that particularly resonate with you.

Notes

Introduction by Allen Carr

Are you tired of so-called experts telling you all the horrible things that will happen to you if you don't quit smoking? What you want is a solution to your smoking problem that works. Believe me, I can sympathize.

I was a 100-a-day smoker who desperately wanted to stop. I knew very well the misery of feeling my willpower give out as my latest attempt to quit failed. I had a permanent cough and regular headaches and chest pains. In short, I knew smoking was killing me but I couldn't find the strength to stop.

Then someone told me I was addicted to nicotine. Up until then I had assumed smoking was a habit I couldn't shake because of something lacking in my physical or mental make-up. I had never thought of myself as an addict. But hearing those words opened a prison door in my mind.

It was an easy step to see my predicament in the same way as I perceived a heroin addict. I wasn't taking the drug for pleasure or as a crutch as I had always believed, I was taking it to relieve the empty, insecure feeling of withdrawal from the previous fix.

Until then I had always feared that if I quit smoking I would be depriving myself of a pleasure or crutch. Now I could see that the "pleasure" was an illusion and nothing more than the partial relief of the misery caused by withdrawal from smoking.

I also saw that my inability to quit was not down to a personal flaw or weakness, it was down to the fact that I was caught in a trap, whereby I mistakenly sought release in the very thing that was holding me prisoner.

The solution was glaringly obvious: all I had to do was stop taking the drug. This was a revelation. I quit straight away, without using any willpower, and I never felt the need or desire to smoke again.

In fact, I immediately went up to my wife and declared, "I'm going to cure the world of smoking."

I couldn't wait to tell other smokers and help them get free of the prison too. I set up a clinic in my house in south-west London and very quickly had to move it to larger premises. Soon I realized that I would never be able to help all the millions of unhappy smokers who wanted to quit in person, so I published my method in a book, *The Easy Way to Stop Smoking*, which remains to this day a global bestseller.

With more than 15 million copies of Easyway books sold worldwide and Easyway clinics treating people in more than 50 different countries, the conclusion is as clear today as it was when I first stopped smoking:

EASYWAY WORKS!

I called the method Easyway because it makes escape from the nicotine trap easy, painless and permanent. Unlike other methods, it requires no willpower and you don't have to endure a traumatic period of withdrawal. All you have to do is keep an open mind and allow yourself to see through the brainwashing that creates the trap.

Anyone can quit with Easyway, as proven by the personal recommendations of millions of happy ex-smokers that have helped to spread the method all over the world. Now is your chance to join them. You hold in your hands the key that will set you free. Carry on reading, carry on smoking. And follow all the instructions.

Allen Carr

HOW THIS BOOK WORKS

This is the first interactive Allen Carr book. Using a pen or pencil on the relevant pages throughout the book, you write the story of how you came to smoke, listing your reasons for doing so and acknowledging your fears about life without smoking. Guided by the text and interactive format, you will come to recognize the truth about your smoking. Record your beliefs, aspirations and insights as you go along. If you follow all the instructions carefully, you then bring the story of your smoking to a close by quitting. That may be hard to believe right now, but please read on. I have only good news for you.

Over the years we have refined and developed the way we apply Allen Carr's Easyway method.

Yet the basic principles remain the same. *Your Personal Plan* is designed to help you quit smoking easily, painlessly and permanently, while you play an active role as you read through the pages.

In each chapter you will find interactive elements: by filling in these elements you will find it easier to cement the key facts in your mind. At any point, you can refer to the summaries at the end of each chapter to reinforce your understanding. By the time you reach the end of Chapter 18, "Your Final Cigarette", you will be ready to enjoy the rest of your life as a happy non-smoker!

If you're sceptical, I don't blame you. All I ask is that you carry on smoking until you feel ready. You have nothing to lose and everything to gain.

Chapter One

Why You Smoke

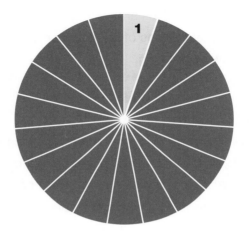

So you're a smoker and you wish you weren't. Join the club! It's a very big club. In fact, every smoker in the world is a fully paid-up member. Seventy per cent of smokers say they wish they could be non-smokers; the rest just don't admit it.

You have admitted it, which is great news. It means you have made the first move in your personal plan to quit smoking. This book will show you how to complete the journey successfully and with ease.

When you reach the end you will be ready to start enjoying the rest of your life as a non-smoker straight away. There will be no need to endure a painful withdrawal period and rather than having a feeling of deprivation, you'll experience a wonderful sense of freedom. What's more, you will achieve all this without relying on willpower.

> *"I've taken control – not because of graphic poster campaigns or shock tactics, but because of John, the Easyway therapist, Allen Carr and me."*
>
> The Irish Times

I'm not going to bore you by telling you that smoking is the world's number one killer, a blight on society that the medical profession has been trying and failing to remedy for decades. You don't need telling that it's antisocial, creates stress, destroys concentration, causes guilt and self-loathing, drives smokers to lie to themselves and other people and costs a fortune. Smokers already know that millions of people die prematurely each year due to it, yet they continue smoking.

WHY?

Understanding why you smoke is key to becoming a non-smoker. There are many reasons why smokers think they smoke, but only one reason why they actually do. As you progress through this book, you will remove all your misconceptions about why you smoke and begin to see the truth. This is your personal plan to becoming a happy non-smoker for the rest of your life.

EASILY
PAINLESSLY
PERMANENTLY

Allen Carr's Easyway organization has been making the same claim to smokers for decades and is constantly inundated with testimonials from happy non-smokers who have found the claim to be true. You can read some of them as you go through the book, and by the end you will be ready to join them.

If you have a smartphone and can use QR codes, you might like to look at some testimonials here or you can use this short web address: http://delivr.com/2n9un

HOW THE METHOD WORKS

As you read through this book, you will be given a series of instructions. In order to succeed, you simply need to follow all the instructions. It's as simple as that. But it's essential that you don't jump to the end, or skip any part of the book. There is no magic word that gives you the cure: Easyway is a method that you need to follow in order, all the way through.

There will be sections where you are required to write notes. Don't worry, it's not an exam and the writing is kept to a minimum. By taking part and adding your own contributions to the plan, you help to ensure that you are following the method and that it's working for you.

> # FIRST INSTRUCTION
> ## FOLLOW ALL THE INSTRUCTIONS

Some smokers, on being told the first instruction, assume the method works by brainwashing them into a new way of thinking. That's half right: by the end of the book you will have a new way of thinking, but it won't be through brainwashing. It's brainwashing that made you smoke in the first place and it's brainwashing that makes you continue to smoke. This method unravels the brainwashing. In other words, it's *counter*-brainwashing.

It achieves that by taking you through a series of steps that help you to see through the illusions that keep you smoking. In order to succeed, all you have to do is follow those steps in order while continuing to smoke until you're asked to stop.

Think of it as being like the combination to a safe. If you don't know the combination, the safe is virtually impossible to crack. If you know the combination but enter it in the wrong order, or leave a number out, the safe will not open. But if you follow the combination in order and in its entirety, the safe will open with ease.

TOO GOOD TO BE TRUE?

Many smokers find the Easyway claim too good to be true, especially when they learn that you can continue to smoke throughout the process. They don't believe it's possible to quit smoking without drawing on all your willpower, or suffering a traumatic period of withdrawal. Such is the grip that smoking has on them. And so they view these claims with suspicion. There must be a catch, right?

Rest assured there is no catch. There is a very simple reason why Allen Carr's Easyway has become such a worldwide success:

THIS METHOD WORKS

In fact, it's smoking that has sprung a catch on you. Without realizing it, all smokers have fallen victim to the most ingenious confidence trick known to man. We're not talking about the tricks the tobacco industry plays to sell its deadly product worldwide. We're talking about the trick played by nicotine itself. The trick that keeps you smoking:

THE NICOTINE TRAP

In order to quit smoking, you need to understand why you smoke. First, let's examine what you think are the reasons you smoke.

"It is a remarkable fact that Allen Carr, on his own admission a non-professional in behaviour modification, should have succeeded where countless psychologists and psychiatrists holding postgraduate qualifications have failed, in formulating a simple, effective way to stop smoking."

Dr William Green, MB, Chb, FRANZCP, MRCPsych, DPM, Head of Psychiatric Dept, Matilda Hospital, Hong Kong

Tick which of the following apply to your smoking:

- ❑ I like the taste
- ❑ I enjoy the ritual
- ❑ It relaxes me
- ❑ It helps relieve stress
- ❑ It's sociable
- ❑ It controls my weight
- ❑ I like the way it looks
- ❑ It helps me concentrate
- ❑ It gives me confidence
- ❑ It's just something I've always done
- ❑ It's a habit I can't seem to shake
- ❑ You only live once
- ❑ I'm exercising my right to choose
- ❑ Smokers are more fun
- ❑ It relieves the craving

You probably didn't tick all the answers. You might even have laughed at one or two of them. These are all reasons that smokers typically give for continuing to smoke.

Whichever boxes you ticked, ask yourself whether you've been fooled into believing they're true when in fact they are nothing more than illusions. All I ask is that at this stage you consider that possibility…

NICOTINE ADDICTION

So let's look at the real reason you smoke. Nicotine is the fastest-acting addictive drug known to man; it takes just one cigarette to get you hooked. In its raw state it is a colourless, oily compound that is highly toxic. Every puff of a cigarette delivers a small dose of this drug that passes into the bloodstream and up to your brain more quickly than an injection of heroin. One cigarette gives you around 20 such doses.

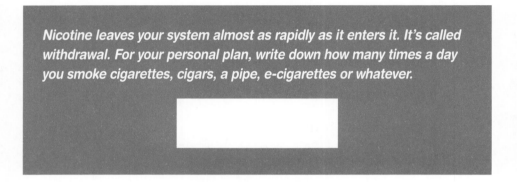

Nicotine leaves your system almost as rapidly as it enters it. It's called withdrawal. For your personal plan, write down how many times a day you smoke cigarettes, cigars, a pipe, e-cigarettes or whatever.

That is the number of times you experience withdrawal.

EVERY SINGLE DAY

Actually, as a smoker you experience withdrawal ALL THE TIME! Remember that for later when we come to talk about withdrawal symptoms.

Many smokers laugh at the term "nicotine addict". They think it's just an exaggerated term for a habit they've fallen into. This implies that they could stop any time they want to. Yet they don't. Or they try to but fail.

TIME AND TIME AGAIN

SPOT THE ADDICT

Which of these would you classify as an addict?

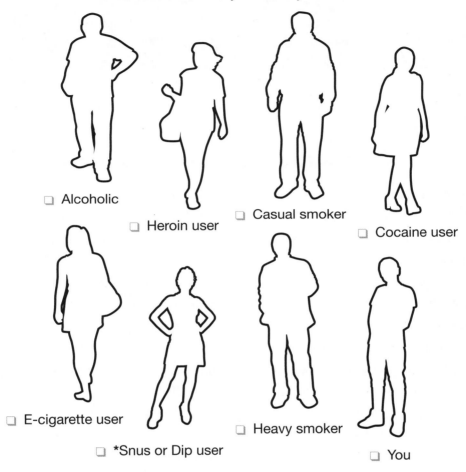

☐ Alcoholic

☐ Heroin user

☐ Casual smoker

☐ Cocaine user

☐ E-cigarette user

☐ *Snus or Dip user

☐ Heavy smoker

☐ You

If you have a basic understanding of addiction, you'll have ticked every box. If you didn't, don't worry. Just make sure you ticked "You". You might want to return later to tick a few more.

---

*Dipping tobacco, aka "Dip", is finely ground or shredded and moistened smokeless tobacco product that is placed between the lip and the gum for extended periods. **Snus** is a moist variant of snuff popular in Sweden. Again it is kept between the lip and the gum.

WHAT DOES SMOKING DO FOR YOU?

Let's look at the question another way. Whenever you light a cigarette, what are you expecting to gain? If you feel like a cigarette now, light one and make a note of what things you're hoping for.

Some smokers say they look to cigarettes for a feeling of satisfaction or stress relief. Others say comfort, relaxation or just a feeling of relief. Some even say they're hoping this will be the last one and they'll never have to smoke again.

The truth is no one smokes to gain anything; you smoke to get rid of something – an empty, insecure feeling. That is the feeling of the body withdrawing from nicotine and it is caused by smoking, not relieved by it!

You know what it's like when a burglar alarm has been ringing all day? Suddenly the noise stops and you experience a wonderful feeling of relief. You haven't gained anything; you've just ended the aggravation of the noise. When you smoke a cigarette, all you're doing is relieving the empty, insecure feeling of your body withdrawing from nicotine. Very soon after you extinguish the cigarette, the aggravation will start again.

SMOKING DOESN'T CURE THE AGGRAVATION, IT CAUSES IT

Non-smokers don't ever suffer this feeling. Think about that for a moment. Do you agree with that statement?

☐ Yes   ☐ No

In her own words: SARAH, London

I was never a heavy smoker. I certainly didn't class myself as an addict. I smoked maybe 10 a day, mostly in coffee breaks and at mealtimes. But every so often, when I wanted to save a bit of money for a holiday or something, I would try to quit smoking for a month or two. I found I could never do it. No matter how much I needed the money, I always found an excuse to keep smoking.

It baffled and frustrated me, because usually I'm determined enough to do anything I put my mind to, but with smoking I felt I was not in control. Then a friend of mine, who was a much heavier smoker than me, told me she'd quit thanks to Allen Carr. It was the explanation of addiction that did it for me. It made me realize that I wasn't smoking because I wanted to, I was smoking because I'd been caught in a trap. And once I understood how the trap worked, it was easy to see the way out.

I quit very quickly and I've had absolutely no desire to smoke ever since.

★ *Recognizing that smoking is an addiction is the first step on your road to freedom.*

★ *As long as you continue to believe that you are in control of your smoking, you will remain in the trap.*

★ *Non-smokers do not suffer from the discomfort that you do.*

Your Story

TO ENJOY WHERE YOU ARE GOING TO – YOU FIRST NEED TO ESTABLISH WHERE YOU ARE NOW!

When people use conventional methods to stop smoking, they're bombarded with information about the health scares and the downsides of smoking. All this does is create fear in the smoker's mind. And what do smokers do when they experience fear? Exactly. They smoke.

The fact is, smokers already know about the downsides of smoking – we spend our lives blocking our minds to them. I want you to stop using this information to scare yourself and simply make a record of where you are in your smoking life and how you got there.

In this short section I'm asking you to be honest about your current situation. The great news is that there is nothing to be scared of. However you describe where you are in your life as a smoker, rest assured I have only good news for you. Escape is at hand. When you consider the health issues and downsides of smoking in this section, you are doing so merely to make a tangible record, like a snapshot photograph, of where you are in your smoking life. I want you to keep this book for the rest of your life. If you ever happen to reflect upon or review this section in the future, I can promise you it will make you smile rather than produce any sensation of fear.

No part of this short section is designed to prevent you from smoking or from convincing you about the principles of Easyway. I've made some pretty sensational and thought-provoking comments to accompany the notes you make as part of 'your story'. I don't expect you to accept them, or agree with them, or be convinced by all of them at this stage. I just ask initially that you merely consider my comments. Trust that every question, every doubt they may provoke in your mind, will be covered by the time you finish this book. This is the starting point of your plan. To enjoy where you are going to you first need to establish where you are now.

At our clinics we begin by looking at each person's smoking story. We don't mean your whole life story, just your smoking story: how you started, how your smoking has grown, why you want to quit, why you've not been able to quit before. It helps everybody to get a clearer picture of their own predicament, and to see that they are not alone.

So let's begin by thinking back to your first cigarette. In the spaces provided, piece together an account of your experience.

When did you have your first cigarette?

Why did you do it?

Who were you with?

How did you find the taste and smell?

How did you feel while you were doing it?

And how did you feel after?

What made you smoke again?

Telling smokers that it's killing them, costing a fortune, controlling their lives, and that it's a filthy, disgusting thing to do does not help them to stop. In fact, it's a waste of time... smokers know that already and find it patronizing.

I KNOW YOU KNOW ABOUT THE HEALTH ASPECTS OF SMOKING. MORE IMPORTANTLY, I KNOW THIS KNOWLEDGE WON'T HELP YOU STOP SMOKING

So this section is private; it's just for you. It's a record of where you stand at the moment. Work through it quickly and honestly, then put it behind you. Then we'll get on with the important stuff: how you can set yourself free!

You've already stated how many you smoke per day, so let's move on to why you want to quit. Think hard about your reasons and enter them in the appropriate spaces provided on the following pages.

MY REASONS FOR QUITTING
Are you worried about the health risks?

☐ Yes   ☐ No

If so, what in particular are you worried about?

Don't worry, we don't focus on health reasons for stopping but there are many good health reasons for quitting. Soon after you stop smoking it's great that you will feel many terrific physical benefits. The coughing, breathlessness, headaches and sinus pains that you come to regard as normal when you're a smoker quickly leave you after you quit.

The human body is miraculous in its ability to recover, and the risk of serious health threats such as cancer and heart disease is significantly reduced when you stop smoking. Perhaps you're already suffering with a serious medical condition. If you think the damage is already done and it's too late, think again.

IT'S NEVER TOO LATE TO QUIT SMOKING

Within minutes of stopping smoking your body begins to heal itself.

The benefits of stopping smoking are obvious, but you might be interested in the following information. It's great to know that you don't have to wait years to start getting the health bonuses from quitting – they start immediately.

20 MINUTES AFTER QUITTING

Your blood pressure and your pulse rate return to normal.

What this means:

Raised blood pressure and high pulse rate both put strain on your heart, increasing your risk of a heart attack. The minute you stop, your risk is reduced dramatically.

8 HOURS AFTER QUITTING

The carbon monoxide levels in your blood are halved.

What this means:

Carbon monoxide from smoking can also produce distortions of time perception, psychomotor and visual impairment and negative effects on cognitive skill. Reducing the level of carbon monoxide in your blood will reduce these problems. Carbon monoxide reduces the uptake of oxygen from the lungs – the higher the levels of carbon monoxide, the lower the levels of oxygen. Oxygen is vital for the functioning of all energy systems in the body; so as soon as you cut carbon monoxide levels, you will experience enhanced energy levels.

24 HOURS AFTER QUITTING

Carbon monoxide is eliminated from the body. Your risk of a heart attack is reduced by half.

What this means:

Well, being half as likely to have a heart attack is great but you can also look forward to better sports performance, with stronger endurance, lower levels of fatigue, improved recovery after exercise and a lower heart rate for each level of exercise.

48 HOURS AFTER QUITTING

99 per cent of nicotine is eliminated from the body.

What this means:

As well as being highly addictive, nicotine has a number of unpleasant side effects on the body. It raises blood pressure, and increases the likelihood of seizures. Get rid of the nicotine and you will get rid of these symptoms.

1 MONTH AFTER QUITTING

Physical appearance improves – skin loses its grey pallor and becomes less wrinkled.

What this means:

You will look and feel much better and other people will soon begin to notice the improvement too.

2–21 WEEKS AFTER QUITTING

Circulation improves.

What this means:

Bad circulation causes numerous problems, ranging from persistently cold feet, slow skin healing, Raynaud's disease and peripheral vascular disease (PVT) which can even lead to limb amputation. Quitting smoking will reduce your risk of most circulation problems.

21+ WEEKS AFTER QUITTING

As years go by your risks of lung cancer and heart attack are massively reduced. 80 per cent of all lung cancer deaths are caused by smoking.

What this means:

YOU ENJOY A LONGER, HAPPIER, HEALTHIER LIFE.

Source: BUPA

Are you worried about the money?   ☐ Yes   ☐ No

Whether you are or not, let's work out what you stand to gain by quitting. This also applies to vaping, snus, patches and other nicotine products. Many nicotine addicts underestimate what they spend.

1. Please calculate your daily spend on nicotine

2. Multiply by 7 for your weekly spend on nicotine

3. Multiply (2) by 52 weeks and write the answer for a year here

When you quit, you will have this much extra cash to spend on genuine pleasures every year.

4. Now write down how many more years you hope to live.

Multiply (4) by (3)

Total

This is the amount you will spend on cigarettes over the remainder of your lifetime if you don't quit now.

THINK OF ALL THE FUN YOU COULD HAVE WITH ALL THAT MONEY!

Don't misunderstand me. Thinking about the money isn't going to stop you smoking, but it's great to work out the bonus you'll enjoy when you do.

It's ironic that most smokers start out thinking smoking makes them look cool, but soon they see the yellow stains on their hands and teeth and begin to feel self-conscious. That's not good for your confidence. The bad breath and stale smoke on your clothes don't help either.

Again, don't misunderstand me. These facts won't help you to stop smoking, but they're great bonuses when you do. The ageing effects disappear and are reversed quickly when you quit.

WHEN YOU QUIT YOU'LL FEEL MUCH MORE CONFIDENT

Do you feel a sense of responsibility towards your loved ones?

Yes   No

Pressure from the people you care about, and who care about you, will drive a lot of smokers to try to quit – or at least pretend they've quit. No parent wants their children to smoke, or to be frightened that they might lose their mum or dad due to smoking. The sense of guilt is immense, especially when you tell them you've quit but are having to sneak off to smoke in secret because your attempt to stop smoking has failed.

This isn't something which will help you stop smoking, but freedom from the guilt and lies is a wonderful bonus when you escape nicotine addiction.

WHEN YOU QUIT SMOKING YOU NO LONGER HAVE TO LIE OR FEEL GUILTY

Are you just bored with being a smoker?

Yes   No

Strange as it may seem to a lot of smokers, some people reach a stage where they've just had enough. They're not particularly worried about the money or the health risks and they're not bothered by how they look. They're just bored with being a smoker and want to be free.

You would think it would be the easiest thing in the world for them to quit, wouldn't you? If smoking was something you did voluntarily, as soon as you stopped feeling you enjoyed it the logical next step would be to stop. And yet they don't stop. Or at least they try to stop but fail. The good news is:

QUITTING SMOKING IS EASY WHEN YOU KNOW HOW

Are you fed up with feeling like a slave to smoking?

☐ Yes   ☐ No

Many smokers don't realize how controlled they were until they quit. But a lot of them do, and find it incredibly frustrating that they keep coming back to doing something they don't even enjoy. Despite countless logical reasons for stopping, they feel incapable, as if they are being forced to smoke against their better judgement.

Of course, nobody forces you to smoke. Nobody holds a gun to your head and says, "Have a cigarette now!" Yet you feel you have no choice because every time you get that empty, insecure feeling of your body withdrawing from nicotine, you find yourself reaching for another cigarette.

This is how nicotine addiction works. It makes the addict seek relief in the very thing that's causing them misery. The massive volume of brainwashing we're subjected to from a very early age leads us to believe that smoking gives us some form of pleasure or a crutch. In fact, it does the opposite, but such is the nature of addiction that it traps us in a prison cell from which we can see no way out, and the harder we try to escape, the more we feel enslaved.

No doubt you still believe you get some kind of pleasure or benefit from smoking. Don't worry, I'll cover that issue shortly.

QUITTING SMOKING MEANS AN END TO THE SLAVERY

Which brings us on to the final part of your story: why you haven't been able to quit up to now. If you can remember, write down how many attempts you have made to quit smoking.

Now write down the longest amount of time you have managed to go before you started smoking again.

And the shortest.

Did your attempts to quit require willpower?

    Yes   No

Did you suffer withdrawal pangs?

    Yes   No

Did you use substitutes, e.g. nicotine patches?

    Yes   No

Did you feel a sense of sacrifice or deprivation?

    Yes   No

Did you "reward" yourself with other "treats", e.g. sweets?

    Yes   No

Did you put on weight?

    Yes   No

Did you become more stressed and irritable?

    Yes   No

Did you try to be a casual smoker?

    Yes   No

If you answered yes to any of these questions, that shows one thing:

YOU WERE GOING ABOUT IT THE WRONG WAY

Sorry if that sounds blunt. I'm sure you put an awful lot of effort into it. But let me make amends by showing you THE RIGHT WAY.

Remember the claim: you can quit smoking easily, painlessly and permanently, without any sense of sacrifice or deprivation, or having to endure any traumatic withdrawal period. What's more, it doesn't require willpower.

ALL OTHER METHODS RELY ON WILLPOWER. COLLECTIVELY I CALL THEM "THE WILLPOWER METHOD"

Imagine you're trapped in a cell sealed by a heavily sprung door. You push on the door but you're pushing on the side where the hinges are. It takes all your effort to open the door a crack and when your strength runs out, the door springs shut again. This is what happens when you try to quit by using willpower.

What you need is someone to tell you to push on the other side of the door, away from the hinges, and it will swing open easily. For anyone who's not in the trap, it's very easy to see the way to escape. But when you're in the trap, it plays an ingenious trick on you, like a mirror that makes everything look the opposite of reality.

THIS IS PRECISELY THE POSITION YOU ARE IN – A TRAP CALLED NICOTINE ADDICTION

It's easy to escape provided you follow all the instructions. First, you need to understand the nature of the trap.

"Any excuse you have will be gone. All your fear will be gone. You will literally have no reason whatsoever to smoke. And you'll love it. Freedom is a beautiful thing. Don't you owe it to yourself to give it a try? What do you have to lose, other than a disgusting addiction?"

Amy, Vancouver, WA, USA

Your Personal Plan

As you approach the end of this book, you will be asked to look back at the last page of each chapter and confirm that you have understood everything you've read. Tick the relevant boxes below, but leave any you are not comfortable with and the very last box unticked. That is for your final flight check at the end of the book. At that time, if you think you've missed anything, go back and re-read the chapter and then tick the remaining boxes.

❏ **There are many good reasons to stop smoking**
❏ **There are no good reasons to continue smoking**
❏ **The only reason I continue to smoke is nicotine addiction**
❏ **Any pleasure or benefit I thought I got from smoking was just an illusion**
❏ **The empty, insecure feeling of nicotine withdrawing from the body is not relieved by smoking; it's caused by it**
❏ **FIRST INSTRUCTION: FOLLOW ALL THE INSTRUCTIONS**

Flight check

❏ **all clear and understood**
Do not tick this box until you are instructed to in Chapter 18.

Chapter Two
The Nicotine Trap

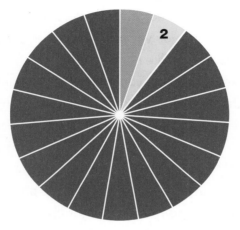

The nicotine trap relies on an ingenious con trick: the ability to make you believe that your worst enemy is your best friend.

SECOND INSTRUCTION

KEEP AN OPEN MIND

If you feel sceptical, don't worry. It's perfectly natural at this stage. In fact, it's important that you question everything as you go through the book. That includes everything you think you know about smoking. Open your mind and the truth will be revealed.

"Allen Carr explodes the myth that giving up smoking is difficult."

The Times

Nobody likes to think they're being conned. You're no fool – you're perfectly capable of detecting when something is good for you and when it isn't. The only reason you indulge in anything that might be bad for you is because you choose to, right?

Well, yes, it's true that nobody forces you to smoke. That is the ingenuity of the nicotine trap – it makes you your own jailer. And enough people have fallen for it to show that this is no ordinary con trick.

MANY HIGHLY INTELLIGENT PEOPLE HAVE BEEN FOOLED INTO BELIEVING THEY NEED CIGARETTES FOR SOME FORM OF PLEASURE OR CRUTCH. AS LONG AS THEY GO ON BELIEVING THAT, THEY REMAIN FOREVER IN THE TRAP

You don't need me to tell you that you have a great deal to gain from quitting smoking. Health, money, appearance, honesty, self-esteem – the arguments against smoking are so strong, and yet millions of people go on ignoring those arguments every day.

WHY?

The only time we think about them is when we attempt to quit smoking; we try to use them as motivation to stop. We focus on what we're trying to escape from, the downsides. But all those factors do is scare us – and what is the first thing smokers do when they experience fear? They smoke!!

Concentrating on the negative aspects of smoking makes it harder to stop, not easier. So ignore the downside for now. Instead, consider the benefits of quitting as wonderful bonuses when you escape to freedom.

IF THINKING ABOUT THE DOWNSIDES OF SMOKING HELPED YOU QUIT YOU'D ALREADY BE A NON-SMOKER

SECURITY OF THE PRISON

There is a common syndrome among long-term prisoners whereby many of them reoffend very soon after being released. The reason they do so is not because they think they can get away with it this time, it's because they miss the "security" of prison. It's what they know, whereas they fear the unfamiliar world of freedom.

This helps us to understand why a smoker with a heavy cough, who clearly gets no pleasure from smoking, continues to smoke. It can be summed up in one word:

FEAR

As a smoker you find yourself in a tug-of-war between two sets of fears. You fear the effects that smoking is having on you, but also fear the prospect of life without what you perceive as your little crutch.

"How will I enjoy social occasions?"

"How will I relax?"

"How will I concentrate?"

"How will I muster the willpower to quit?"

"How will I cope with the trauma of withdrawal?"

"How will I cope with stress?"

 **LIFE AS A NON-SMOKER**

Take a few minutes to think about your fears with regard to quitting. What do you think you'll miss? List your answers below.

> *Be completely honest. At this stage it's quite normal to believe that quitting will involve sacrifice. It doesn't matter how many things you list; whether it's one or 21, it's something we need to look at more closely.*

1 ....

2 ....

3 ....

4 ....

5 ....

6 ....

7 ....

8 ....

9 ....

10 ....

11 ....

12 ....

13 ....

14 ....

15 ....

16 ....

17 ....

18 ....

19 ....

20 ....

21 ....

THE TUG-OF-WAR OF FEAR

In the tug-of-war of fear, why is it smoking that so often wins out? Why do smokers end up taking their chances with the likelihood of what smoking might do to them?

There are two answers:

1. Smokers bury their heads in the sand.
When it comes to the health hazards associated with smoking, they tell themselves, "It won't happen to me," whereas they see the things they fear in life without smoking as unavoidable.

2. Smokers don't choose to take their chances with smoking.
They are compelled to keep smoking by their addiction to nicotine.

The tug-of-war is created by the false belief that smoking does something for you, i.e. it gives you some kind of pleasure or a crutch, and that quitting is incredibly hard. Take away that belief and you take away the fear of quitting.

IN FACT BOTH ENDS OF THE TUG-OF-WAR ARE CAUSED BY ONE THING... CIGARETTES

The fact is that most smoking is done without any thought whatsoever. Smokers don't savour every drag. The only time we are really conscious of smoking is when it's causing us misery or when we're not allowed to smoke. What kind of pleasure is that? When you're doing it you're either not aware that you're doing it, or you wish you weren't doing it.

IT'S ONLY WHEN YOU CAN'T DO IT THAT SMOKING SEEMS SO PRECIOUS

BRAINWASHING

So where do these false beliefs come from? Why do we think we get something positive from smoking? There are many influences that contribute to us believing that smoking gives us pleasure or a crutch. It's that belief that has us convinced that quitting is hard.

Parents
Medical professionals
Peer groups
Tobacco advertising and product placement
Other smokers
Ex-smokers
Anti-smoking groups

The last two in the list may surprise you. But most of us have met a "reformed" smoker who can't wait to tell you about the agony they went through to quit, and the daily challenge they face in remaining a non-smoker. You're hardly likely to think quitting is easy after hearing all that. These people convince us we'll never be free!

Anti-smoking groups too insist on constantly claiming that quitting is hard and requires immense reserves of willpower, as well as substitutes to wean you off nicotine. They also perpetuate the myth that smoking is a habit, a pleasure, a crutch and that focusing on the negative aspects will help you quit.

Using the QR code or short website address, you can find out what Sir Richard Branson and other celebrities have to say about Allen Carr's Easyway. http://delivr.com/2n7np

The nicotine trap is like the conman who steals the slates off your roof and then offers to sell them back to you.

When we light our first cigarette, we let nicotine into our body for the first time. When we stub out that cigarette and nicotine leaves the bloodstream, it creates a very slight empty, insecure feeling, which is barely perceptible but enough to make you feel something's missing. It's this feeling that smokers are always looking to relieve.

WE SMOKE TO RELIEVE THE FEELING CREATED BY THE FIRST CIGARETTE

Because the slight discomfort is caused by nicotine withdrawal and smoking puts nicotine back in the system, the cigarette does create a temporary feeling of relief, which we misinterpret as pleasure. But as soon as we stub out the cigarette and the nicotine begins to withdraw again the uneasy feeling returns.... and so a lifetime's chain of misery begins.

SMOKING DOESN'T RELIEVE THE DISCOMFORT, IT CAUSES IT!

It's essential that you understand this point completely. Like all addictions, the nicotine trap works by fooling its victims into believing they can find relief in the very thing that's causing them misery.

Read this page again until you are completely clear on this point and then confirm it by ticking this box.

We'll look at how the illusion of pleasure, crutch and relief develops later, but at this point we just need you to understand how it begins.

THE PHYSICAL FEELING

But just how bad is the feeling of withdrawal from nicotine? In the last chapter, on page 24, you wrote down how many times you smoke each day. This means your body starts to withdraw from nicotine the same number of times. If you're a chain smoker, you don't let the withdrawal go very far before you light up again. But what happens at night when you go to sleep? Do you writhe around in agony from the withdrawal symptoms as you go through the night without smoking?

> **Next time you feel the desire to smoke, make a point of thinking about the feelings, both physical and mental.**

The physical feeling of withdrawal is so slight that most smokers aren't even aware of it. They experience a little pang, a mild, empty, insecure feeling, which prompts them to start thinking about their next smoke. Easyway calls this feeling:

THE LITTLE NICOTINE MONSTER

The Little Monster is so weak as to be almost non-existent. It doesn't bother us when we're asleep because we are not conscious of it. Only when we are conscious does it become a problem, because it arouses another, bigger monster, which lives in our mind.

> **At one time in your life you may have believed in fairies and Father Christmas. When you discovered they did not exist, could you go back to believing in them again?**

THE BIG NICOTINE MONSTER

Your addiction to smoking is 1 per cent physical and 99 per cent mental. This 99 per cent is the Big Monster – the brainwashed part of your mind that interprets the tiny cry of the Little Monster as "I want a cigarette". Of course, if you have a cigarette all you will do is feed the Little Monster.

KILLING THE LITTLE MONSTER IS EASY

It's because smoking addiction is 99 per cent mental that nicotine patches and gum don't work. They only address 1 per cent of the problem. All you have to do is stop putting nicotine into your body and it will quickly die. Killing the Big Monster is where smokers who quit with the willpower method fail.

This method does not require willpower. The aim of Allen Carr's Easyway is to destroy the Big Monster by unravelling all the brainwashing that has kept you in the nicotine trap.

In order to escape the trap you need to correct your understanding. That is something entirely within your control. You have a choice. You can feel miserable at the thought of never being allowed to smoke again, or you can feel excited and elated at the prospect of never having to smoke again and, more importantly, that you are all set to find it easy.

THIRD INSTRUCTION
··
START OUT WITH A FEELING OF EXCITEMENT AND ELATION

Your Personal Plan

I have read and understood the following points about the nature of the nicotine trap:

❏ **SECOND INSTRUCTION: KEEP AN OPEN MIND**

❏ **Fear keeps smokers in the trap**

❏ **It's only when I can't smoke that smoking seems precious**

❏ **I smoke to relieve discomfort caused by the previous cigarette**

❏ **Addiction is 1 per cent physical (the Little Monster) and 99 per cent mental (the Big Monster)**

❏ **THIRD INSTRUCTION: START OUT WITH A FEELING OF EXCITEMENT AND ELATION**

Flight check

❏ **all clear and understood**

Do not tick this box until you are instructed to in Chapter 18.

Chapter Three

The Myth

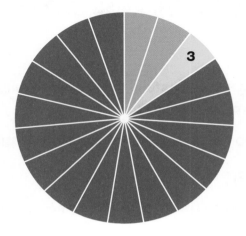

In this chapter you will learn how, when presented with two conflicting views, it's easy to separate the truth from the illusion. Once you see the situation as it really is, escape from the trap becomes easy.

Don't worry if you feel sceptical at this stage. Scepticism is good; it means you will question everything until it's clear in your mind. But don't let your scepticism prevent you from opening your mind to the possibility that this method will work for you. After all, what have you got to lose?

OUR EXCUSES FOR SMOKING KEEP CHANGING, BUT THE ACTUAL REASON NEVER DOES

THE REAL REASON WE SMOKE IS TO TRY TO END THAT EMPTY, INSECURE FEELING THAT THE FIRST CIGARETTE CREATED

CIGARETTES CAUSE THE CRAVINGS; THEY DON'T RELIEVE THEM

In Chapter One we listed the common reasons smokers give for smoking and asked you to tick the ones that apply to you. Look at that list again and tick the ones that you still agree with.

- ❑ I like the taste
- ❑ I enjoy the ritual
- ❑ It relaxes me
- ❑ It helps relieve stress
- ❑ It's sociable
- ❑ It controls my weight
- ❑ I like the way it looks
- ❑ It helps me concentrate
- ❑ It gives me confidence
- ❑ It's just something I've always done
- ❑ It's a habit I can't seem to shake
- ❑ You only live once
- ❑ I'm exercising my right to choose
- ❑ Smokers are more fun
- ❑ It relieves the craving

You are two chapters and a bit in and already you will be starting to question some of the boxes you may have ticked.

Most of the time we smoke without even thinking about it. When we do stop and think about it, we begin to see through the myths.

In his own words: MARK, Glasgow

I started smoking when I was 15 and I remember my first cigarette like it was only yesterday. I was with a friend from school who lived round the corner and we were out on our bikes. He pulled out a couple of cigarettes that he'd pinched from his mum and he lit one, took a tentative drag and passed it to me. I put it to my lips and I remember breathing in too hard – I took a great lungful of smoke and spent the next five minutes choking and gagging.

It was the most disgusting thing I'd ever tasted, but my friend was laughing at me and holding the cigarette out for me to try again. I felt ashamed so I took it and had another couple of puffs.

Next time we went out cycling together he brought a whole packet and we sat and smoked together. I felt proud that I was getting used to the taste and I felt grown up, sitting there mimicking the way I'd seen smokers take the cigarette from their lips and flick the ash off.

Within a couple of weeks I would say it felt like I had started to enjoy the taste and when I went to parties I found smoking made me feel more confident and relaxed. I started buying my own cigarettes and began to realize the cost of my newfound "pleasure". Despite numerous attempts to quit, I remained a smoker until the age of 35, when my first child was born. I didn't want her breathing in my toxic fumes.

I looked for a method that would help me kick what I thought was a "habit" I couldn't shake, and I discovered Allen Carr's Easyway. The first thing they told me was that smoking isn't a habit, it's an addiction. That opened my eyes and I quit after one session at the clinic.

Mark's story is a very familiar one. What is remarkable about it is how our perception of the cigarette changes over time, going through these states:

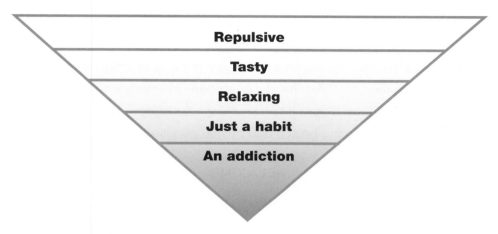

Repulsive

Tasty

Relaxing

Just a habit

An addiction

Where on that scale are you?

The smoker's perception of the cigarette changes, from the most repulsive thing they've ever tasted, to an acquired taste, to a relaxing, confidence-boosting support, to something they just do out of habit, to an addiction. Yet the cigarette doesn't change, and neither does the real reason why the smoker continues to smoke after those first unpleasant puffs:

IT'S CALLED NICOTINE ADDICTION

> *Around 10 million adults in the UK are smokers: 21% of men and 19% of women. Children are more likely to smoke if their parents smoke and parents' attitude to smoking is an important factor in whether young people take up smoking or not.*

The smoker's change in perception from repulsion as he or she smokes more is easy to explain.

TASTY

Mark's pride in acquiring the taste for cigarettes was actually misguided. He hadn't acquired anything; he had overridden his senses and lost the protective mechanism that told him smoking was poison. His body had built up a tolerance to the poison and he had acquired a LOSS OF TASTE.

RELAXING

The reason Mark felt relaxed and confident when smoking was because he felt unrelaxed and insecure when he was not. These uncomfortable feelings were caused by smoking the previous cigarette and the nicotine leaving his body. Smoking only partially relieves that feeling so he would never have felt as relaxed and confident as he would as a non-smoker.

JUST A HABIT

When smokers stop saying they enjoy it or it gives them confidence, and excuse themselves by saying, "It's just a habit," they have reached a point where they sense smoking is not giving them the pleasure or crutch they once thought it did and they can't understand why they still do it.

AN ADDICTION

Only the first and final perceptions are accurate: smoking is repulsive and the only reason you continue to do it is nicotine addiction. The rest are all factors in the myths that create the Big Monster.

If it's that easy to change your mindset in favour of smoking, it's just as easy to change it back… if you know how.

INSTINCT V INTELLECT

The acquired loss of taste is an example of how our intellect overrides our instincts to our detriment. Most animals rely on instinct for survival and humans are no different. Fear, pain, hunger, revulsion – these are just four examples of the unconscious reactions that help us to avoid danger from predators, injury, starvation and poison. But unique to man is his intellect, which enables us to reason and rationalize and pass on understanding. It also, however, enables us to override instinct. Mark's reaction to that first puff on a cigarette was instinctive. His body convulsed in an effort to reject the poison. Had he heeded his instincts he would not have taken another puff. But his intellect told him there was reason to persevere, and over time his body continued to reject the poison but also built up a tolerance to it.

Every now and then, maybe when you haven't had a cigarette for a while, have you noticed how a cigarette makes you feel lousy/tired/a little sick? Did it ever occur to you that's because your body is trying to reject the poison?

Intellect is a marvellous thing. It gives mankind innumerable advantages over the rest of the animal kingdom. But if our intellect is fed with false information, a myth, it can be a hugely destructive force.

SOCIETY PROGRAMMES FUTURE GENERATIONS TO BECOME DRUG ADDICTS

We have no need to smoke before we fall for the nicotine trap, but once we are in the trap we face repeated situations that we perceive as triggers for a cigarette. Having been convinced that smoking helps us to relax, concentrate, relieve boredom and stress and to feel more confident, we automatically reach for a cigarette in a multitude of circumstances. Of course, we sense that the cigarette relieves discomfort (caused by nicotine withdrawal) and this fools us into believing it helps us to relax, to concentrate, to overcome boredom, beat stress and feel confident.

The more we experience it, the greater our belief that cigarettes help us, hence the sense of relief when we light up a cigarette.

UNRAVELLING AN ILLUSION

Our task is to replace the misinformation about smoking – the myths that are still making you tick some of the boxes on page 51 – with the correct information, and thus get you back to that blissful state of never wanting or feeling the need for a cigarette that you had before you became a smoker.

Your second instruction was to keep an open mind. We are bombarded with so much brainwashing about smoking that a simple statement like

NO SMOKER ENJOYS SMOKING

can seem like the words of a lunatic. All our lives we have been fed images of happy people smoking cigarettes. But just open your mind to the possibility that that statement above is true.

After all, what is there to enjoy? The foul taste? The vile smell? The damage it does to your health and wealth?

YOU'RE NOT EXPECTED TO ACCEPT EVERYTHING THIS BOOK TELLS YOU AT THE FIRST TIME OF ASKING

QUESTION IT, EXAMINE IT, AND LOOK AT IT FROM ALL ANGLES UNTIL YOU KNOW WITHOUT ANY DOUBT THAT YOU ARE SEEING THE TRUTH

Just make sure you do the same with everything you think you know about smoking. The truth will soon appear, and once you see the real picture, you will never be fooled again.

On the next page is an exercise to show you how easy it is to rejig your mind from one firmly held belief to a different belief based on fact.

Exercise

Here are some irregular black shapes. Look hard at the black shapes. Do you see a message?

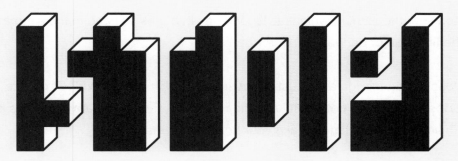

At first, it might look like a random line of building blocks. If so, look again. This time look at the shapes with your eyes half closed (through your eyelashes) and you can make a word appear. It might help if you move your head back a little (or to one side) and look again from a distance. You should see the word "STOP".

The word hasn't suddenly appeared; it's been there all along. If you couldn't see it that's because you thought you were looking at an irregular black shape. After all, that is what you were told. So you were focusing on the black rather than the shapes around it.

The nicotine trap works in a similar way; it makes you focus on the inverse of reality.

Once you can see the word "STOP", however, you will always be able to see it. The same principle applies to the truth about smoking:

ONCE YOU SEE THROUGH THE ILLUSION, YOU WILL NEVER BE FOOLED BY IT AGAIN

WHAT'S WRONG WITH BELIEVING ILLUSIONS?

If the brain can be deceived into believing that smoking gives us pleasure or a crutch, does it matter that it isn't true?

Consider the ostrich, which, as legend has it, buries its head in the sand at the first sign of danger.

Does the danger go away just because the ostrich can't see it? Of course it doesn't. Are you better off knowing the truth? The stakes are high. This is life and death. It's time to take your head out of the sand.

> *Every single smoker is likely to die prematurely as a direct result of their smoking. It's not just the shortening of life, it's the early deterioration of the QUALITY of life.*

Aside from the constant fear from the threat to your health and wealth, the nature of addiction is to send the addict into a downward spiral of misery. We end up knowing we're just pathetic drug addicts.

THE ONLY THING THAT CAN STOP THE DOWNWARD SPIRAL IS TO STOP TAKING THE DRUG

Notes

THE VOID

Insecurity is a natural human state. From the shock of coming into the world to the uncertainty of adolescence, to the responsibilities of adulthood, we are prone to an empty, unsupported feeling that drives us to look for reassurance. Brainwashed by the myth that smoking offers comfort, relaxation and a strong identity, most youngsters try it sooner or later.

As the nicotine leaves the body, a new void opens up as we experience withdrawal. The second cigarette goes some way to filling it and a secure, satisfying sensation results. The nicotine trap has claimed another victim. All the smoker "enjoys" is feeling like a non-smoker. The cigarette just removes the bad feeling caused by the first cigarette.

With each withdrawal, the void gets bigger so the smoker has to take larger and larger doses to get any sense of relief. They don't realize that the only way to get complete relief is to stop smoking.

The more we buy into the belief that the cigarette gives us something, the more we are compelled to smoke. The natural tendency is to smoke more as we get older; this is the nature of addiction.

Exercise

Next time you smoke a cigarette, pay close attention to how it makes you feel.

Does it relax you completely?   ❏ Yes ❏ No   ❏ Maybe

Do you achieve a sense of total contentment?

❏ Yes ❏ No   ❏ Maybe

Does the feeling last for long?   ❏ Yes ❏ No   ❏ Maybe

Do you understand that it just got rid of the discomfort caused by the previous cigarette?   ❏ Yes ❏ No   ❏ Maybe

Do you understand that that cigarette has merely created yet another feeling of discomfort, that it created a problem rather than relieved one?   ❏ Yes ❏ No   ❏ Maybe

THE PITCHER PLANT

The descent into addiction involves an ingenious trap that is all the more deadly for its subtlety. It's like that wonder of nature, the pitcher plant, which attracts insects with the sweet smell of nectar and then draws them down into its carnivorous chamber.

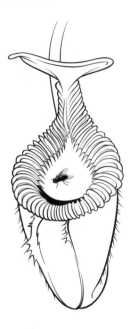

When the fly first lands it has no idea of the danger. All it cares about is the sweet nectar and it knows it can fly away whenever it wants. But why should it want to?

The nectar is delicious. So the fly ventures further into the plant, consuming more and more of the nectar, until it finds itself slipping in. It tries to scramble back towards the light but it's so engrossed with the nectar that it misses its chance to escape.

It continues to feast as it slides in and then, too late, it realizes that it's being consumed by the plant, rather than the other way round.

By the time the fly realizes it has a problem, it's already too late. It's trapped.

When did you realize you were trapped? There's one important difference between you and the fly. The fly is doomed. But you can escape. Read on. I have only good news for you.

The lure that draws victims into the nicotine trap is far more subtle than the nectar on the pitcher plant. It isn't sweet and delicious, it's foul-tasting and smelly and causes physical revulsion.

Funnily enough, as youngsters this convinces us we'll never get hooked. Do you remember thinking that?

We're convinced that smokers must get something out of it, otherwise why would they put up with it?

Without this brainwashing, everybody would stop after the first puff.

From that point on, the nicotine trap is just like the pitcher plant. Smokers don't realize they're in a trap – yet they clearly are. Some smokers never realize.

IT'S ONLY WHEN YOU TRY TO QUIT THAT YOU SEE YOU'RE IN A TRAP

IT'S NEVER TOO LATE TO ESCAPE

The nicotine trap is not a physical trap, it is a mental one. No one else is keeping you imprisoned. That is part of the ingenuity of the trap.

It uses the myths to make you your own jailer. But that is also its weakness. You can escape any time you choose. All you need to do is correct your perception and the trap will spring open.

ESCAPE IS EASY!

Exercise

Try to perceive yourself as a non-smoker sees you.

Unless you're a heroin addict, the idea of injecting yourself with heroin probably fills you with horror. Think about why heroin addicts have the desire to stick a needle in themselves. It's terrible to watch them going through the devastating process of withdrawal, or witness the trauma and desperation of them wanting their next fix.

Do you envy them their desire? Or do you pity them, relieved that you don't have to go through the same torment, and wish you could help them see their addiction for what it is: a downward spiral of misery?

A non-smoker would look at you in much the same way.

The lengths you go to feed your addiction; the state you get into when you have to go without; the money you waste; the damage you do to your health; the pathetic promises to quit that never come to anything; the feeble submission to abject slavery.

Take some time to look at yourself from a non-smoker's point of view. Be honest. Describe how you think they see you... as someone controlled by a drug.

Your Personal Plan

I have read and understood the following points about the smoking myth:

- ❑ The nicotine trap makes smokers believe the inverse of the truth

- ❑ Smoking is not an acquired taste – it's an acquired loss of taste

- ❑ Smoking doesn't make me relaxed and confident – the addiction makes me insecure and shaky

- ❑ The only thing that can stop the downward spiral of misery is to stop smoking

- ❑ It's never too late to escape

- ❑ Escape is easy (don't worry if you remain sceptical about this, just accept the possibility that it might be true)

Flight check

❑ **all clear and understood**

Do not tick this box until you are instructed to in Chapter 18.

Chapter Four
First Steps to Freedom

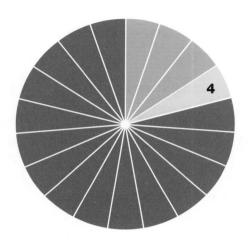

You're making good progress towards becoming a happy non-smoker. It's essential that you are clear about the marvellous gains you are about to make and remove any doubts from your mind. In order to bring about the necessary change in your mindset, you need to remove the desire to smoke – you need to kill the Big Monster.

The Big Monster interprets the cries of the Little Monster as "I want a cigarette". In fact, it interprets many other signals in the same way: hunger, nervousness, tiredness, excitement, relaxation and stress.

These are all instinctive signals your body needs something specific: food, relaxation, security, sleep, adrenaline, comfort, fight and flight. Only the addicted mind would interpret these signals as a need for nicotine.

Smokers suffer the empty insecure feeling of nicotine withdrawal their entire lives. Non-smokers never suffer it and that's one of the great bonuses of being free.

It's imperative that you kill the Big Monster because even after the Little Monster is dead, the instinctive signals of hunger, tiredness, nervousness, excitement, relaxation and stress will continue to be sent to your brain for the rest of your life. If the Big Monster is still there interpreting them as "I want a cigarette", you will be faced with two options:

Option 1: Crack and start smoking again, returning to lifelong misery

Option 2: Live the rest of your life in torment, craving a cigarette.

These are your two options when you quit with the willpower method. But Easyway helps you kill the Big Monster by unravelling the brainwashing. You have already seen how the nicotine trap creates an inverse reality. You are beginning to see through the illusions. These are your first steps to freedom.

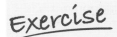

Exercise

Turn back to page 51. Are there any answers you would like to change?

"It didn't take any willpower. I didn't miss it at all and I thank God every day that I am free."

Ruby Wax

THE DIFFERENCE BETWEEN SMOKERS AND NON-SMOKERS

Why do you think it's so easy for smokers to see the obvious solution for the poor heroin addict but not for themselves? Why is it that you can look at yourself through the eyes of a non-smoker and see what smoking does to you, yet when you look through your own eyes it's not that simple?

It comes down to the fundamental difference between a smoker and a non-smoker.

DESIRE

Non-smokers have been subjected to the same brainwashing as smokers and part of that will have been absorbed. Many people who have been non-smokers all their lives will still believe the myth that smoking gives you some kind of pleasure or a crutch, but they still make a decision not to inflict the world's number one killer on themselves.

They are able to do this because, unlike the smoker, their judgement has not been affected by addiction.

The difference between smokers and non-smokers is that non-smokers have not had the brainwashing reinforced by the addiction.

OF COURSE YOU FEEL BETTER AFTER SMOKING A CIGARETTE! YOU'RE A NICOTINE ADDICT!!

But remember, each cigarette you smoke perpetuates the misery. It doesn't relieve it.

The aim of this book is not just to help you quit smoking. Many people succeed in quitting, only to start again at some later date. Our aim is to help you quit permanently and, more importantly, to ensure that you become a HAPPY NON-SMOKER.

Most smokers will agree that the arguments against smoking outweigh the arguments in favour, yet they continue to smoke.

From time to time this awareness will prompt them to attempt to quit, but if they try with the willpower method they nearly always fall back into the trap again because, regardless of the arguments for and against, they still harbour the desire to smoke.

THIS METHOD DOES NOT REQUIRE THE POWER OF REASON TO OUTWEIGH THE TEMPTATION TO SMOKE. IT REMOVES THE TEMPTATION ALTOGETHER

Only by doing that can we ensure that you become a non-smoker and remain one.

PERMANENTLY

Non-smokers have no desire to smoke and neither did you until you tried those first experimental cigarettes.

It's only nicotine addiction that creates the desire to smoke – the Big Monster in your brain that interprets the tiny cries of the Little Monster as "I want a cigarette".

Let's examine this temptation to smoke more closely.

WHAT SMOKING DOES FOR YOU

We've looked at what you think smoking does for you, now let's examine the facts, starting with:

SOME OF THE NEGATIVES

Highly addictive

Costs a fortune

A powerful poison

World's number one killer

Causes lethargy, breathlessness and lowered immunity

Destroys the nervous system

Reduces courage, confidence and concentration

Causes severe coughing and wheezing

Tastes and smells awful

Makes exercise difficult and unappealing

Stains the teeth, lips and hands

Causes wrinkles

Causes bad breath

Ruins our skin and complexion

Induces shame and guilt

Ages us prematurely

Encourages other family members to smoke

THE POSITIVES

THERE
ARE
NO
POSITIVES

That's right, smoking does absolutely nothing for you whatsoever.

IT DOESN'T EVEN GIVE YOU A HIGH!

Some smokers disagree and say it sometimes makes them feel dizzy. That's not a high!! It's caused by oxygen starvation and poisoning. If you like "dizzy" so much by all means spend time spinning around in circles!! It doesn't cost a fortune, it won't control your life and it won't kill you… but to be honest, it isn't much fun, is it?

Why is it so easy to see the negatives of heroin addiction, yet smoking seems so attractive? The answer is in your living room. Next time you settle down to watch a movie or drama on TV, keep this page open and make a note every time you see someone smoking. Think about how smoking is portrayed: is it a positive or negative image?

Programme	Positive	Negative
	☐	☐
	☐	☐
	☐	☐
	☐	☐
	☐	☐
	☐	☐
	☐	☐
	☐	☐
	☐	☐
	☐	☐
	☐	☐
	☐	☐
	☐	☐
	☐	☐

If you think tobacco advertising has been banned, think again. TV and cinema are doing a tremendous job of perpetuating the myth that smoking gives you pleasure. The contrast with the way heroin is portrayed is stark.

HEROIN	SMOKING
ADDICTION	COOL
POVERTY	AFFLUENCE
SQUALOR	GLAMOUR
SLAVERY	HAPPINESS
DISEASE	POWER
WEAKNESS	TOUGHNESS
DEATH	COURAGE

Now make a note every time you spot one of these incidents in a movie or drama on TV:

- SMOKER'S COUGH

- NICOTINE-STAINED HANDS

- YELLOW TEETH

- A HEROINE REFUSING TO KISS THE HERO BECAUSE HIS BREATH SMELLS (OR VICE VERSA)

- A SMOKER PANICKING BECAUSE HE'S RUN OUT OF CIGARETTES

- A SMOKER'S LOVED ONE BEING FEARFUL FOR THEM

- THE SMOKER'S BEHAVIOUR AND MOOD BEING DICTATED BY THEIR ADDICTION

- THE RATTLING SMOKER'S LAUGH

THE TRUE FACTS ABOUT SMOKING ARE SELDOM PORTRAYED ON SCREEN

When you stop and take note of the way smoking is portrayed, the bias becomes obvious. Just like the "STOP" illusion in the last chapter, once you see what's going on it seems obvious.

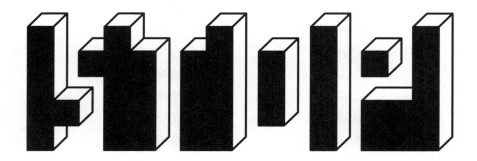

But in everyday life we don't stop to analyze what we're being told, especially when it comes from a trusted source, like TV or the medical profession. We just absorb information without really examining it.

And thus we develop a twisted perception of smoking – a perception that is presented to us by people with a vested interest in our continuing to smoke.

Now that you've started to examine the information you receive about smoking, you are on your way to clearing your mind of the myths and seeing the real picture.

This change in mindset is the key to ending your addiction to nicotine.

Whenever you think about smoking, instead of wanting a cigarette and feeling deprived because you can't have one, you can rejoice in the knowledge that you are free and have no desire to smoke.

WHAT HAVE YOU GOT TO LOSE?

In order to achieve the mindset that will set you free from the nicotine trap, you must kill the Big Monster. To do that, you must first address the chief ally of addiction:

FEAR

Many smokers, when asked why they don't quit, reply that they're afraid they won't be able to. The fear of failure holds them back.

Think about that logically. If you try to quit, what is the worst that can happen? You fail and remain a smoker. If you don't try, you GUARANTEE that you remain a smoker.

Choosing to remain a smoker because of the fear of failure is illogical. You are, in effect, fearing a calamity that has already happened: you are a smoker!

The fear of failure can be put to good use. Actors use it to make sure they learn their lines; athletes use it to drive them to train harder; and you can use it to help you succeed. Use it to open your mind to the truth.

The fact that smokers fear failure to quit proves that they don't like being smokers and the idea of remaining a smoker for life fills them with despair.

THINK POSITIVE!

You won't fail if you follow all the instructions. So put the fear of failure out of your head and focus on all the positive gains you stand to make by becoming a non-smoker.

FOURTH INSTRUCTION
NEVER DOUBT YOUR DECISION TO QUIT

THE FEAR OF SUCCESS

Why would anyone fear success? For the same reason a long-term prisoner fears the freedom of life on the outside. It depends on your perception of "freedom".

For many smokers, quitting suggests a lifetime of deprivation and misery. They have been brainwashed into believing they will be making a terrible sacrifice.

Without their little crutch, life will be full of insecurity and they'll never be able to enjoy living in the way they do now.

They'll give it a try for the health benefits and the money, but deep down they're already looking forward to failing.

Rest assured, everything in life gets better when you become a non-smoker.

You suffer less stress, you are better able to handle setbacks, you have more energy, you become more relaxed and happy, you value yourself more highly, you perform better in social situations – the list goes on and on.

THINK POSITIVE!

YOU HAVE ABSOLUTELY NOTHING TO FEAR FROM QUITTING SMOKING, ONLY MARVELLOUS GAINS TO LOOK FORWARD TO

 **Exercise**

CHANGE YOUR WAY OF THINKING

As an exercise, turn back to page 43 and remind yourself of the fears you wrote down with regard to quitting. Now take each point in turn and try to imagine a positive alternative: e.g. "I will enjoy mealtimes more because I won't be itching to get out for my next cigarette."

Use this page to write down your positives.

1 ....
2 ....
3 ....
4 ....
5 ....
6 ....
7 ....
8 ....
9 ....
10 ....
11 ....
12 ....
13 ....
14 ....
15 ....
16 ....
17 ....
18 ....
19 ....
20 ....
21 ....

The fear of success is based on our, and other smokers', experiences when we used the wrong methods to attempt to quit smoking. Start to imagine life as a non-smoker in a positive light and you will start to feel very excited about what you are about to achieve.

For a moment ponder the positives you wrote down on the previous page and allow your imagination to roam. Look forward to the freedom from slavery, the confidence of knowing you no longer feel you need cigarettes in order to enjoy life, and remind yourself that cigarettes never helped you to enjoy life in the first place. On the contrary, they made it worse.

WHEN YOU STOP SMOKING YOU'LL FIND THAT BAD TIMES BECOME EASIER AND GOOD TIMES BECOME EVEN BETTER

The third instruction was to look forward to quitting with a feeling of excitement and elation.

It's essential that you follow this instruction and remove any sense of doom and gloom. You are on your way to a much happier way of life.

> *On average, it has been estimated, that for every cigarette you smoke, your expected lifespan will be reduced by 11 minutes. US Centers for Disease Control and Prevention estimate that adult male smokers lose 13.2 years of life and female smokers lose 14.5 years of life because of smoking.*

These statistics fail to tell the whole story. It's the drastic negative impact on the quality of life which is equally disturbing. Has your quality of life already been harmed by smoking? Can you feel your body is already paying a price? This doesn't get better; it just gets worse. These facts shouldn't scare you; they're reasons to be cheerful. That's because **YOU WILL SOON BE FREE!**

Your Personal Plan

I have read and understood the following points about my first steps to freedom:

❑ It's essential that I destroy the Big Monster that makes me think I get some kind of pleasure or a crutch from smoking

❑ The difference between smokers and non-smokers is that non-smokers do not suffer the discomfort caused by cigarettes and nicotine withdrawal

❑ Smoking does absolutely nothing for me whatsoever

❑ The fear of failure proves that I hate the thought of remaining a smoker for life

❑ The fear of success disappears when I unravel the brainwashing and see through the illusions

❑ FOURTH INSTRUCTION: NEVER DOUBT YOUR DECISION TO QUIT

Flight check

❑ **all clear and understood**

Do not tick this box until you are instructed to in Chapter 18.

Chapter Five
The Illusion of Pleasure

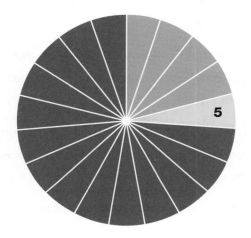

The second instruction was to keep an open mind. It's important that you accept smoking does absolutely nothing for you whatsoever. It's only addiction and brainwashing that make you think it does.

The temporary and partial relief from nicotine withdrawal creates the illusion of pleasure, but it is no more a genuine pleasure than the relief of taking off tight shoes after a day of walking around. Would you deliberately wear tight shoes just to get that relief?

Just as nobody has ever enjoyed wearing tight shoes,

NO SMOKER HAS EVER ENJOYED SMOKING

There's no reason to feel deprived. You're not making a sacrifice as you're not giving up a genuine pleasure or crutch.

ROLL UP, ROLL UP!

Imagine a sharp-dressed salesman trying to sell you a magical potion. This potion, he claims, will increase your powers of concentration and relieve boredom. It will ease stress and aid relaxation. You will love the taste and smell and you'll be delighted with the way it enhances your sex appeal.

Oh, and it will help you lose weight too, and make you the life and soul of any party.

Would you believe him? Or would you brand him a charlatan?

The tobacco industry has been spinning the same yarn for decades and smokers have been lapping it up. But you don't need a particularly open mind to see that there's something fishy about a product that claims to help you concentrate and also claims to help you switch off, chill out and feel carefree a few moments later. In fact, you need a particularly closed mind not to see it.

THE PANIC OF ADDICTION CLOSES YOUR MIND TO THE TRUTH

When you see through the illusion, the panic disappears. That's when you rediscover what it's really like to be truly relaxed.

"Hi Mr Carr! I'm writing a paragraph about your book since it's my bible. I carry it with me as a reminder of what I was before and how good I feel today. Thank you."

Heidi Karppinen, Sweden

Exercise

So instead of accepting the myths, let's really examine the things that are supposed to be enjoyable about smoking.

TASTE

Smoke a cigarette now and concentrate on the taste. Remember how your first cigarette tasted. How hard did you have to persevere to "acquire" the taste? In fact, you didn't acquire the taste, you became immune to it. How does the cigarette taste now?

Do you like the taste?	☐ Yes	☐ No

SMELL

Many smokers believe they enjoy the smell, yet they can't stand the smell of other smokers' cigarettes or stale smoke. Non-smokers find the smell repulsive. If you really do enjoy the smell, is that reason enough to keep smoking? A lot of people like the smell of roses but it wouldn't bother them if they never smelt another rose in their life.

Do you like the smell?	☐ Yes	☐ No

The novice smoker's revulsion at the taste and smell of cigarettes is an instinctive reaction, designed by nature to protect us from poison. By persevering we override our instincts and the body responds with its next protective mechanism: it builds up a tolerance.

Subsequently, the taste and smell don't repel us so violently and we begin to associate them with the "relief" of nicotine withdrawal, which we perceive as a pleasure.

This creates the illusion that we actually like the taste and smell.

The cigarette after a meal is often claimed as tasting "better" yet it's the same cigarette out of the same packet. It's the taste of the meal that's special.

SPECIAL CIGARETTES

Do you have certain cigarettes that you look forward to and consider to be special?

☐ Yes   ☐ No

Most smokers will insist that some cigarettes taste or feel better than others. These are their special cigarettes, the ones they associate with certain times of day or certain events, such as after a meal or with a drink.

Here's a list of the special cigarettes most commonly cited among smokers who attend our clinics. Tick the ones that apply to you, and add any other personal favourites at the bottom.

❑ The first of the day

❑ With a morning coffee or tea

❑ After a meal

❑ With a drink

❑ During a work break

❑ After shopping

❑ After exercise

❑ After sex

❑ Other ....
....

Now look closely at this list. Can you see anything in common among all the special cigarettes mentioned?

There are two common factors that connect the occasions smokers associate with special cigarettes, and neither of them has anything to do with the way the cigarette tastes.

1. They all follow a period of abstinence

The reason these cigarettes appear especially satisfying is because the Little Monster has been getting really quite impatient for its fix, and so the relief feels greater than usual. If you've been unable to smoke or you've been putting it off until you reach a certain time or place, the Little Monster will have been crying for longer than usual and the Big Monster will be getting irritated. That "ahhh" feeling when you light up is nothing more than keeping the two monsters quiet.

2. They mostly coincide with situations which non-smokers enjoy too

No one associates special cigarettes with hard times. Is the cigarette you smoke when you're caught in the pouring rain special? What about the one you smoke just before a visit to the dentist?

Special cigarettes are nearly always associated with times that would be enjoyable even without the cigarette: a break, a rest, a social occasion, a time to reflect on a job well done, after sex. As a nicotine addict you're incapable of enjoying these moments without cigarettes. That's not an argument "for" smoking; it's one of the biggest arguments "against".

When you quit smoking you will discover that all such occasions are actually MORE ENJOYABLE WITHOUT A CIGARETTE.

For example, imagine how good you would feel after an exercise session, when you pat yourself on the back for the work you've put in AND congratulate yourself for having no desire to ruin that healthy glow by smoking.

In his own words: BEN, London

I used to be a 20-a-day smoker but there was always one cigarette that stood out as the one I looked forward to. I would smoke it in the pub with a pint of beer and I would just feel myself unwinding. As soon as I got to the end of the working day I would be looking forward to that cigarette, but I would never be tempted to smoke it before I got to the pub. It wouldn't have been the same. If I had to work late, I would wait until I got out, reached the pub, bought my pint and found myself a seat. It was always the same pub, always the same beer and, if possible, always the same seat. If someone had taken the cigarette away from me at that moment I would probably have fought them to get it back.

But then they changed the law so I could no longer smoke inside the pub and had to go outside. It just wasn't the same. The fact that it was winter didn't help, but the whole scenario that I had held so dear was undone. I found it quite depressing and I realized that smoking wasn't giving me any pleasure any more. So I quit. But I still missed that favourite cigarette.

About a month after quitting, I was walking past the pub with a colleague after work and he asked if I wanted to go in for a pint. I was driving so I couldn't drink but I agreed to join him and ordered an orange juice. As we sat down and chatted, I was amazed to find I got the same feeling of unwinding that I'd always attributed to the cigarette and the beer. In fact, it felt better because I had no desire for a cigarette.

STRESS

The empty, insecure feeling of the body withdrawing from nicotine is a form of stress. When you put more nicotine into your body, that stress is partially relieved. This is why smokers believe that nicotine relieves stress. In fact, it is a primary cause of stress. Non-smokers don't suffer the additional stress caused by nicotine withdrawal; therefore, smoking actually adds to your stress.

STRESS	=	NICOTINE WITHDRAWAL + "I WANT A CIGARETTE"

Imagine a smoker and a non-smoker experiencing a stressful day. They're identical people with identical lives apart from the smoking Assess the stress levels as the stress builds up.

	NON-SMOKER	SMOKER
8am: They have an argument with their partner	Stress 1	Stress 1
9.30am: Their car breaks down on the way to a job interview	Stress 2	Stress 2
10.30am: They're nervous about the interview ...	Stress 3	Stress 3
10.35am: "I WANT A CIGARETTE"		Stress 4*

*Additional stress cause by nicotine withdrawal and feeling of "I want a cigarette"

WHO HAS MORE STRESS AT 10.35AM? The non-smoker is at stress level 3, yet the smoker is at stress level 4. The smoker lights a cigarette and partially relieves the cigarette-related stress. Yet smokers remain more stressed than non-smokers. The smoking-related stress is only partially relieved when they light a cigarette. How sad that smokers become convinced that smoking helps them with stress. **CAN YOU SEE HOW THE CON TRICK WORKS?**

THE SLIPPERY SLOPE

Just as rats develop an immunity to rat poison, humans build an immunity to addictive poisons like nicotine. This immunity acts as a protective buffer, so that next time you take the poison it doesn't have quite as much impact. In order to get the same effect, therefore, you have to increase the dose. This explains why smokers increase the amount they smoke from those first unpleasant puffs and are always having to fight the urge to smoke more. The graph below shows how this decline takes place. Like the fly's descent into the pitcher plant, the smoker always craves something more, and the more you crave, the further you fall. Below, the graph shows a smoker's level of wellbeing as he goes through life. The smoker's descent below 100 per cent begins when he stubs out the first cigarette and nicotine withdrawal begins. It's an empty, insecure feeling, almost imperceptible.

WELLBEING

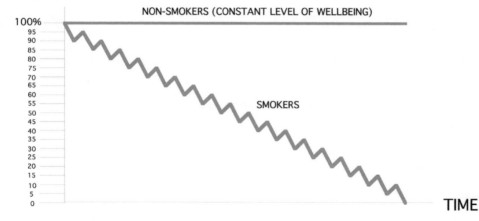

There are genuine highs and lows and stresses and strains in life, but for the purposes of this exercise and for the sake of clarity, we're going to ignore those and focus exclusively on the effect that smoking has on your level of wellbeing over time.

We're going to assume that before you get hooked, you're on

100%. Being on a high means having no problems. As a smoker, you're permanently below 100% – i.e. below the level of wellbeing you would have had if you were a non-smoker – because you're constantly withdrawing from nicotine but you're not aware of it because it's so slight and you regard that state as normal.

Assume you're ten points below because of the Little Monster and you recover five of those points when you light up. You will receive a little boost, but you're still below the level of a non-smoker. Perhaps you're thinking, "So what? Won't that five-point gain make me feel better, even if it's an illusion?"

Would you put on tight shoes just for the relief of removing them? This is what all drug addicts effectively do, but only because they don't understand the trap they're in. As time passes and you go through life as a smoker, you slide further and further down as your wellbeing declines both physically and mentally.

At first it doesn't bother us as we think we can stop whenever we like. But as you go deeper and deeper into the pit, terrible things start to happen. You become lethargic and short of breath.

A wheeze and a cough develop. Those cancer scares change from being remote impossibilities to looming larger and larger at the back of your mind. You realize you're not smoking just when you choose to and that cigarettes are now controlling your life.

You've got to have them and you sense you're spending your hard-earned money not for a genuine pleasure or crutch but just to be a slave and to risk horrendous diseases.

Your wellbeing level is therefore gradually but continuously declining and the "high" you come back to when you light a cigarette is going down in proportion.

The great news is that when you quit you quickly return to the level of wellbeing you would have had all your life if you had never lit that first cigarette.

THE RITUAL

Some smokers say the thing they love about smoking is the ritual: the opening of the packet, the offering round, the handling of the cigarette, the lighting up… they make a big show of their favourite lighters and ashtrays.

IT'S ALL NONSENSE

The ritual is not why you smoke. If it is, why not make one tiny but significant alteration? Why not leave the cigarette unsmoked? You can still have all the fun with the packet and the lighter, just don't bring the cigarette to your lips and light it.

You might as well tell someone who's gone out to a fancy restaurant not to eat the food. By all means enjoy the décor and the table setting, unfold the napkin, peruse the menu, discuss the wine list and share a joke with the waiter. But let's face it, what you're really there for is the food.

The same is true of the smoker. Forget the ritual, what you're really doing it for is to get the nicotine. It's no different from junkies injecting heroin. They don't do it because they like injections. It's to get the drug to which they're addicted.

> **The ritual is just another attempt to glamorize what we know is a filthy, antisocial and lethal addiction.**
>
> **Do you believe you enjoy the ritual of smoking?**
>
>   ☐ Yes   ☐ No

HABIT

Many smokers know that smoking gives them no pleasure but they assume it must have some hidden benefit that keeps them craving it subconsciously. So they shrug their shoulders and call it a habit.

"It's just a habit I've got into."

> **Do you have any other habits? If so, make a list of them here. They could be good habits, like taking a half hour walk each evening, or bad habits, like biting your nails. Don't include anything that involves outside influences, such as alcohol, food or other people.**

Now choose one of your more regular habits and ask yourself, "Could I quit this if my life depended on it?"

When we attempt to quit smoking with willpower, the "habit" of smoking can create trigger moments – the impulse to light a cigarette. At these times we attempt to fight the impulse using willpower and normally fail, so we end up smoking.

With Easyway, the same habitual impulse or trigger moment does nothing more than act as a wonderful reminder that you're free. Because you don't feel deprived, you're happy with these moments and have no need to battle them. Does this sound too good to be true? Read on.

The words "habit" and "addiction" are often interchanged but this is misleading. Habits are not controlled by external influences – you are in control.

Smokers think they are in control of their smoking and they think they should be able to stop and start whenever they choose. The fact that they fail to do so makes them feel weak and foolish.

They don't realize that the only reason they smoke is because they are hooked on an addictive drug.

The "hidden benefit" that they think keeps them smoking is not a benefit at all, it's an illusion – the illusion that smoking gives you some kind of pleasure or a crutch and that quitting will mean pain and sacrifice.

You can bring an end to a habit through willpower.

With an addiction, you don't need willpower, you need understanding – the understanding that you are not in control but that you are controlled by an addictive drug. The drug controls you through

FEAR

Fear is the chief weapon of

ADDICTION

Replace the drug with this understanding and you regain control.

Do you smoke out of habit?	Yes	No

Your Personal Plan

I have read and understood the following points about the illusion of pleasure:

❑ The association with the relief of nicotine withdrawal creates the illusion that I like the taste and smell of cigarettes

❑ So-called "special" cigarettes seem precious because they follow a period of abstinence and coincide with occasions that would be enjoyable anyway

❑ Smoking doesn't relieve stress, it is a primary cause of stress. It's important to understand how I've been tricked into believing the opposite

❑ The tendency is always to smoke more, not less. Anyone who tries to curb the amount they smoke is always fighting this urge

❑ The only way I can remove the urge to smoke is to quit completely

❑ The smoking ritual is just an attempt to glamorize a filthy addiction. It's not why I smoke

❑ Smoking is not a habit, it's an addiction

Flight check

❑ **all clear and understood**

Do not tick this box until you are instructed to in Chapter 18.

Chapter Six

Why Willpower Doesn't Work

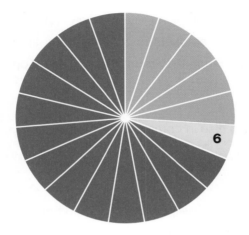

Many smokers find it hard to believe that they can quit without willpower. The fact is, if you rely on willpower you're actually more likely to fail, as we will explain in this chapter.

You've probably heard the saying, "You'll never quit smoking unless you really want to," or something along those lines. This is often interpreted, by smokers and non-smokers alike, as meaning you need to draw on all your reserves of willpower in order to quit.

But there is a much easier way, based on the same saying:

CHANGE YOUR MINDSET. REALIZE THAT YOU DON'T GET ANY PLEASURE OR CRUTCH FROM SMOKING AND YOU CAN BECOME A HAPPY NON-SMOKER, INSTANTLY, PAINLESSLY AND PERMANENTLY

The reason smokers think quitting demands huge amounts of willpower is because they are not convinced that they really want to quit. And one of the reasons they're not convinced that they really want to quit is because they think it will demand huge amounts of willpower.

It's another aspect of the smoking myth, which is perpetuated by everyone from hardened smokers to vehement anti-smoking campaigners. Whichever side of the fence they're on, they all agree on one thing: quitting isn't easy.

They have something else in common:

THEY'RE ALL WRONG

If quitting were a matter of willpower, you would have to conclude that the reason millions of people try and fail to quit every year is because they are weak-willed. That would suggest that the vast majority of smokers are weak-willed, since all but a tiny minority of smokers have tried to quit at some time in their lives.

Aside from the fact that this is statistically unlikely, a quick look at some typical smokers proves it to be nonsense.

Easyway has helped millions of people from prominent professions: doctors, lawyers, business owners, actors, singers.

Do you think these people would have got where they are if they had been weak-willed?

Think back to your first cigarettes: how hard did you have to push yourself to overcome the revulsion until the taste and smell didn't bother you any more? And which of your friends was it that started smoking first and introduced you to smoking? Didn't it tend to be the confident, dominant ones?

Think about the really heavy smokers you know. Do you consider them weak-willed? And what about the idols who sold you the image of smoking in the first place?

WEAK-WILLED PEOPLE DO NOT TEND TO BECOME SUPERSTARS

If you ran out of cigarettes late at night, how far would you walk for a packet? A mile? Two miles? How much willpower does that take?

And since smoking was banned in public places, what lengths have you gone to to keep it up? A weak-willed person would have conceded defeat when they found they were no longer allowed to "enjoy" their special cigarettes in pubs or restaurants. Most smokers stubbornly picked up their drink and went outside – even in the middle of winter!

"I just stopped. Not because it [smoking] causes cancer, not because it smells nasty, not because anyone disapproves. I stopped because Allen Carr explained why there is no point continuing. He employs pure logic, a logic so logical that it's magical. He never judges, criticizes or nags. He just understands, and explains."
Victoria Coren, professional poker player, journalist and TV presenter

In her own words: DILLY, Hoboken

I've always prided myself on my determination and my courage to stand up for myself in difficult situations. I'm sure people who know me would call me strong-willed. I'm only 4ft 11 tall but I make up for it with my personality. I don't take any nonsense from anybody.

When I started smoking, I thought it added to my sense of power. I persuaded myself I felt confident with a cigarette in my hand, like those professional women you see in movies who boss all the men about and run the show. I loved that image, but one day I found myself standing outside work in the rain, trying to smoke a damp cigarette, and I suddenly felt very foolish. If any of my staff had seen me my aura of power would have been blown.

So I decided it was time to quit. I went back to my desk and threw my remaining pack of cigarettes in the trash. I lasted until the following morning. By 9am I had a new pack and I had smoked my way through three. I felt disgusted with myself and threw the pack away again. The next morning I bought another one.

I couldn't understand what was wrong with me. Why didn't I have the strength to stop and remain that way? Why was I allowing cigarettes to control me? I didn't realize then that it was actually my strength of will that was keeping me smoking.

Despite all the arguments for stopping, I didn't really believe them. The thought of being a non-smoker made me panic and, because I was addicted, what I really believed was that I wanted to keep smoking. So that's what I did until I found Easyway.

THE MISERY OF THE WILLPOWER METHOD

The fear of success prevents a lot of smokers from even trying to quit. They have been convinced that life as a non-smoker will be one of sacrifice, deprivation and misery. Ask any smoker who has quit with the willpower method and that's the story you're likely to get.

Using willpower will not make you a happy non-smoker for the rest of your life. It will make you a miserable ex-smoker, always one puff away from falling back into the trap.

You only require willpower if you have a conflict of wills. The climber who wants to reach the summit but is faced with a yawning crevasse needs willpower to overcome his fear of falling and to overcome exhaustion.

When you quit smoking, you only have a conflict of wills if you still harbour a desire to smoke. The desire to smoke comes from the belief that smoking gives you some kind of genuine pleasure or a crutch.

Smokers who use willpower to quit believe they are sacrificing this pleasure or crutch, and so they feel a sense of deprivation that opens up like a crevasse that they will never get over. Rather than rejoicing in the knowledge that they need never smoke again, they become miserable at the thought that they can't.

The more strong-willed they are, the more they prolong the misery. Take away a child's sweets and it will go into a tantrum, a self-imposed state of misery. Which child will continue its tantrum longer, the weak-willed or the strong-willed? The strong-willed are more likely to prolong their agony. Which means that, ironically, strong-willed smokers often find it harder to quit with the willpower method.

REINFORCING THE ILLUSIONS

Think back to the section on special cigarettes in the last chapter. Those cigarettes all seem special because they come after a period of abstinence. While the Big Monster remains alive in your mind and you still have a desire to smoke, the longer you go without smoking, the more precious the next cigarette will seem.

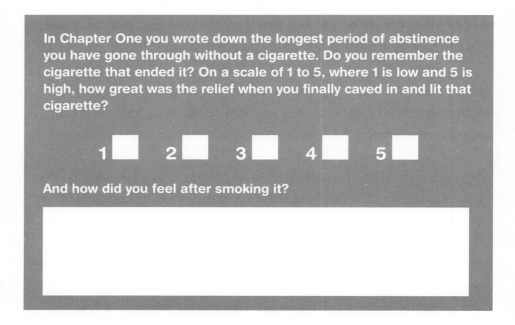

In Chapter One you wrote down the longest period of abstinence you have gone through without a cigarette. Do you remember the cigarette that ended it? On a scale of 1 to 5, where 1 is low and 5 is high, how great was the relief when you finally caved in and lit that cigarette?

1 ☐   2 ☐   3 ☐   4 ☐   5 ☐

And how did you feel after smoking it?

Most people feel terrible after the cigarette that ends their attempt to quit. It comes as a tremendous relief when they light it because it ends a prolonged period of self-imposed misery, but it also confirms them as a failure. The conflict of wills is never clearer than at this moment.

The effect can be devastating, forcing smokers deeper into the nicotine trap than they were before and convincing them that they will never have what it takes to quit.

WAITING FOR NOTHING

With the willpower method, how do you know when you've succeeded? You fight the desire to smoke with all your will, hoping that one day the desire will disappear. But the longer you deny yourself, the more precious smoking becomes and the stronger your desire for the next cigarette. You never know when the urge to smoke might become too much for you but you hope it never will, so you spend the rest of your life waiting for something not to happen.

With Easyway you can enjoy absolute certainty the moment you stub out your final cigarette. Remove the desire to smoke and quitting becomes easy. You don't have to wait for anything. You can get on straight away with enjoying life as a happy non-smoker.

Notes

Your Personal Plan

I have read and understood the following points about why willpower doesn't work:

❑ Smokers are not weak-willed. On the contrary, it takes a strong will to continue to smoke in the face of so many good reasons to stop

❑ Using willpower will not make me a happy non-smoker for life

❑ You only require willpower if you have a conflict of wills

❑ Unless you understand the illusion of pleasure, the next cigarette (the one you can't have) will always seem precious

❑ With the willpower method you are always waiting for something not to happen, so you're left forever wondering if you've succeeded

Flight check

❑ all clear and understood

Do not tick this box until you are instructed to in Chapter 18.

Chapter Seven
No Sacrifice

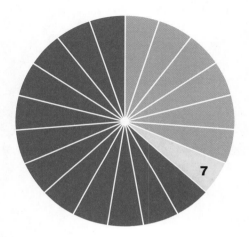

Smokers who try to quit and fail, regardless of which method they follow, all fail for the same reason: they believe they are making a sacrifice.

When you try to quit with the willpower method, this belief is reinforced, often by the very people who are encouraging you to quit. You only need willpower if you have a conflict of wills.

It is the belief that smoking gives you some kind of pleasure or a crutch that creates the tug-of-war of fear.

With Allen Carr's Easyway, the desire to smoke is removed altogether, so there is no feeling of deprivation.

It's essential that you get it absolutely clear in your mind:

YOU ARE NOT GIVING UP ANYTHING

Can you remember how many times you've tried to "give up" smoking?

Write the figure here

Box 1

Now write how many times you've succeeded

Box 2

On page 37 you wrote down your record for the longest and shortest amounts of time you've managed to quit. Write those figures again here.

Longest

Box 3

Shortest

Box 4

In box 2 you should have written 0. Success means quitting permanently. It need only happen once. The fact that you're reading this book suggests you have never succeeded in quitting smoking.

This page is a reminder of what happens with the willpower method. You can quit for a long time or a short time, you can quit numerous times, but you always end up smoking again. You always end up back in the trap.

In fact,

WITH THE WILLPOWER METHOD YOU NEVER ESCAPE THE TRAP

BAD INFLUENCES

The clue is in the expression "give up". Smokers who try to quit with the willpower method talk about "giving up" because they genuinely believe they are making a sacrifice. They know and understand the many good reasons for quitting but they still think they're going to be deprived of a pleasure or crutch.

You need to be wary of ex-smokers who have quit with the willpower method and are still fighting the temptation to smoke, because these are among the worst culprits for spreading the myth that quitting involves a sacrifice.

They fall into two camps: the "Holier Than Thous" and the "Whiners".

HOLIER THAN THOUS

Holier Than Thous, or HTTs, are easy to spot. They're the ones who, as soon as they've stubbed out their last cigarette, put up "No Smoking" signs in their homes and cars. They invite smokers to their homes just so they can forbid them to smoke, and so they can gloat.

HTTs become avid campaigners for spreading the word about the damage smoking does to your health and wealth and they'll tell you how they find it incomprehensible that an intelligent person like you finds it necessary to put those filthy things into your mouth and set light to them. In fact, they are far more ferocious in their attacks on smoking than people who have never smoked. They seem to forget that they did exactly the same thing for years.

Do you know anyone who fits this description?
Write their names here:

WHINERS

The Whiners are those smokers who, as soon as they hear you've quit, come up to you, shake you by the hand, wish you success, tell you how much healthier and wealthier you'll be, assure you that you've made the right decision… and then tell you how they quit years ago but still miss it terribly.

Whiners love to let everyone know they've quit and they love to tell you what a sacrifice they've made. For anyone who has just summed up the willpower to quit, the effect is devastating. You're pinning your faith on the hope that one day you'll wake up without the desire to smoke. Whiners shatter that hope.

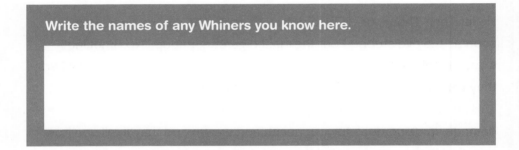

Write the names of any Whiners you know here.

Beware of ex-smokers who have quit with the willpower method. The reason the HTTs like to rail against smoking and the Whiners like to reminisce is because they have never overcome their addiction. They still believe they have made a genuine sacrifice. Their Big Monster is still alive.

HTTs and Whiners have a negative effect on smokers because they reinforce the misconception "once a smoker, always a smoker". They confirm the fear that you might stop smoking but you can never be completely free.

Imagine how these tortured souls feel when they finally succumb to temptation and smoke again. The relief must be immense. The longer you force yourself to resist the desire to smoke, the greater the relief when you don't have to force yourself any more.

Anyone who has tried and failed to quit with the willpower method will know this feeling of relief, but can you remember ever feeling, "Great, I'm so glad I'm a smoker again! This cigarette tastes gorgeous!" On the contrary, the relief is marred by a feeling of failure and foreboding and the cigarette is always a disappointment, tasting rather like the first cigarette you ever smoked – repulsive. Don't get me wrong: the sensation of relief is huge, but that's like wearing tight shoes just for the relief of taking them off.

ALL DRUG ADDICTS ARE LIARS, INCLUDING SMOKERS

The truth is, when you quit smoking you are not "giving up" anything, you're gaining something marvellous:

FREEDOM FROM ADDICTION

Remember, the aim of this method is not to help you resist the temptation to smoke, it is to remove the temptation altogether.

YOU'RE GETTING RID OF A DISEASE

In his own words: STEVE, Dingwall

I tried to quit countless times, always more in hope of a miracle than actual belief that I could succeed. I just didn't believe it was possible to stop smoking and be happy because I'd never met anyone who had done it. Or I thought I hadn't.

I was talking about it one day with a workmate who didn't smoke and I said to her, "You're so lucky you've never been a smoker." Her reply stunned me. "Don't be silly," she said, "I used to smoke 40 a day!"

I'd known her for three years and I had always assumed she'd never been a smoker. She wasn't like any ex-smoker I'd ever met before. So I asked her if she ever felt tempted to smoke again and she said, "You have to be joking! I don't miss it at all."

It was like a door opening in my mind. For the first time I believed that it was possible to quit and be happy because the evidence was there right in front of my eyes. Thanks to this discovery, when I came to quit with Easyway I was more than ready to believe that I could become a happy non-smoker.

HAPPY NON-SMOKERS

> **Write down the names of all the happy ex-smokers you know.**

The chances are this will be a shorter list than your list of HTTs and Whiners, not because they are rare, but because people who are happy not to be smoking don't tend to make such an issue of it. They just get on with their lives so that, like Steve, you might assume they've always been non-smokers.

There are happy non-smokers all around you, and Easyway has played a significant part in adding to their number. Carry out your own research. Ask people who you assume to be lifelong non-smokers if they've ever smoked. You might find a few surprises.

Add them to your list.

If you've got a smartphone use the QR code to watch video clips of happy ex-smokers who used Easyway to quit. If you haven't got a smartphone don't worry, you can use this short web address: http://delivr.com/2zmjg

As any happy non-smoker will tell you, you don't give up anything when you quit, but you do spare yourself something. In fact, you spare yourself a lot of things.

The slavery of addiction

The drain on your finances

Consumption of a powerful poison

Exposure to the world's number one killer

Grey complexion and dull skin and eyes

Lethargy, breathlessness and lowered immunity

Degradation of your nervous system

Reduced courage, confidence and concentration

Constant coughing and wheezing

The awful taste and smell

Stained teeth, lips and hands

Premature aging and wrinkles

Bad breath

Fear of cancer

Shame and guilt

Guilt about family and loved ones afraid for you

15% of high school boys in the US use smokeless tobacco. Smokeless tobacco contains 28 cancer-causing agents. Adolescents who use smokeless tobacco are more likely to become cigarette smokers.

Happy non-smokers are proof that there is nothing to give up when you quit smoking. They have discovered that any pleasure they thought they got was a con trick and that the reality is life gets much more enjoyable when you stop.

If you're afraid that you won't be able to quit without becoming an HTT or a Whiner, look at your list of happy non-smokers and remind yourself that there is nothing to fear.

YOU DON'T NEED CIGARETTES – THEY DON'T GIVE YOU ANY PLEASURE

If you're still not convinced that you can remove the desire to smoke, go back and re-read Chapter 5 until you understand that any pleasure or crutch that you think smoking gives you is an illusion, brought about by your addiction to nicotine and a lifetime's brainwashing.

See through the illusion and ending the addiction is easy. Unless, of course, you think you're different to everybody else.

"I smoked for 15 years and regretted every day of it. I could not quit. Thank you for showing me I can do it! To anyone out there thinking they can't do this, you can!"

Andrew H, NJ, USA

Your Personal Plan

I have read and understood the following points about the illusion of sacrifice and deprivation:

❏ I am not "giving up" anything

❏ I am getting rid of a disease

❏ With the willpower method you never escape the trap

❏ I will beware of ex-smokers who've quit with the willpower method

❏ I have everything to gain and nothing to lose by stopping

Flight check

❏ **all clear and understood**

Do not tick this box until you are instructed to in Chapter 18.

Chapter Eight

The Addictive Personality

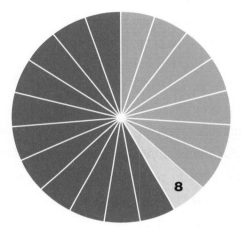

The theory of the addictive personality offers no solution to smokers who want to quit. All it does is make smokers feel helpless. They feel trapped.

GREAT NEWS
ANY SMOKER CAN QUIT WITH EASYWAY
IT HAS NOTHING TO DO WITH YOUR PERSONALITY

"Normally when we have health or fitness gurus of any sort on this show they are greeted with great scepticism, but I have to say our switchboard is jammed and every single caller is positive about Allen Carr. It is quite amazing."

Julian Warricker, BBC 5Live Radio

Some smokers accept that they are addicted to nicotine and appear to understand everything they are told about the trap and how it is easy for smokers to get free, yet when it comes to their own smoking, they think that a different set of rules apply.

They believe they are doomed to be forever addicted because of something in their genetic make-up. The addictive personality theory gives smokers another excuse to keep smoking.

"I can't help it; it's the way I'm made."

"Twenty-four years after stopping smoking, I'm still advocating Allen Carr's book and the mental approach it encourages. I have seen many individuals use this book to get free of cigarettes – not just free of smoking, but mentally free of the habit too."
Dr John Briffa BSc MB BS, Medicine, author and health journalist

THE THEORY

The addictive personality theory is based on the fact that some addicts are addicted to more than one thing. Alcoholics, for example, are often heavy smokers, as are heroin addicts.

The theory is reinforced by the fact that smokers tend to share certain physical characteristics: the grey complexion, the dull eyes, the nervous fidget, the lethargy, the dry wrinkled face... The theory concludes that there are certain types of people who are genetically predisposed to addiction. Some studies even claim to prove it.

Even if you did have an addictive personality or some kind of genetic predisposition to addiction, it doesn't mean you have to be an addict. You weren't an addict before you became addicted, so there's no reason why you can't go back to being the happy non-smoker you were before you started smoking. This method makes it easy for ANY smoker to stop.

THE STATISTICAL ANOMALY

If the addictive personality theory was an important factor and a certain proportion of the world's population were genetically predisposed to smoking and other addictions, you would expect that proportion to remain fairly constant over time. Evolution is a slow process. You wouldn't expect any major changes in the way we're made in the space of just one century.

Yet the statistics tell a different story. In Western Europe and North America, smoking has declined over the last 75 years, while in Asia it has increased massively. In the 1940s in the UK, for example, over 80 per cent of the adult male population was hooked on nicotine. Today it's under 25 per cent.

Are we supposed to believe that this genetic predisposition to addiction has migrated almost wholesale out of Western Europe and America and into Asia?

It really doesn't matter whether or not you have some kind of genetic predisposition to addiction if such a thing exists; you'll still find it easy to stop and to stay stopped.

Notes

THE SYMPTOMS OF POISONING

Those physical traits that seem to bind all smokers together are joined by a sense among smokers that they are one distinct breed. Smokers like to flock together, they seek one another's company and seem to be more relaxed when they're united.

This is one reason why smokers fear becoming non-smokers – they think it will put them outside their social group. But wait – there's a contradiction here. If all smokers are one and the same, why should your smoking be different to anyone else's? If all smokers are of a kind, doesn't that mean that if one can quit they all can?

The fact is, individual cases are irrelevant.

ALL SMOKERS ARE THE SAME

You become an addict because you took an addictive drug. Smokers prefer the company of other smokers because it makes them feel less self-conscious. It also means there are always likely to be cigarettes on hand. And they develop similar physical traits because they are all poisoning themselves with nicotine. Their tendency to lack moderation in other areas of their lives is simply what happens after their body and mind are controlled by a drug.

Nicotine addiction is the cause, not the effect.

Anyone can be cured of nicotine addiction but there is only one way to do it. Stop taking nicotine.

In order to stop painlessly and permanently, you have to understand that smoking, vaping or any other way of taking nicotine does absolutely nothing for you whatsoever.

WHY DO SOME SMOKERS SEEM MORE HOOKED THAN OTHERS?

Anyone can be seduced into smoking a cigarette for the first time. When you smoke your first cigarette, you're hovering on the rim of the pitcher plant and you step on to the slippery slope.

Some people descend very slowly into the trap and never realize they're hooked. Others plunge in headlong and become chain smokers almost immediately.

Why you smoke a second cigarette and, if you do, how quickly you then slide down the slippery slope depends on a number of different influences.

Some people are less susceptible to the brainwashing, and so they never smoke that second cigarette.

The foul taste and smell of the first one is enough to put them off for life.

Others may be more determined to "acquire" the taste and may build up a tolerance faster due to their physique. Some smokers restrict the amount they smoke because of lack of money, or opportunities to light up.

There are countless different factors that influence whether you become a smoker and how heavy a smoker you become, but an addictive personality is not one of them.

> ★ *One of the best things about escaping the nicotine trap is feeling free from that empty, insecure feeling that smokers believe is part of their make-up.*

> ★ *It's not your personality or your genetic make-up that addicts you, it's the drug.*

Your Personal Plan

I have read and understood the following points about the addictive personality theory:

❏ All smokers are the same

❏ I became an addict because I took an addictive drug, not because of my personality or genetic make-up

❏ Anyone can be cured of nicotine addiction. I just have to stop taking nicotine

❏ Many factors influence how heavy a smoker you become. Personality is not one of them

Flight check

❏ all clear and understood

Do not tick this box until you are instructed to in Chapter 18.

Chapter Nine
Driven to Distraction

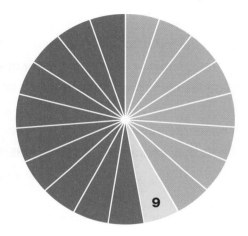

Many smokers firmly believe that smoking helps them to concentrate. This is another illusion created by the addiction to nicotine. It takes a simple truth – that smoking destroys your concentration – and turns it on its head.

Before you start reading this chapter, make sure you haven't smoked for some time – longer than you would normally go between cigarettes. We need to examine your state of mind.

"Some friends of mine who had stopped, using Allen Carr's method, suggested I tried it. I did. It was such a revelation that instantly I was freed from my addiction. Like those friends of mine, I found it not only easy but unbelievably enjoyable to stay stopped."

Sir Anthony Hopkins

The myth that smoking helps you to concentrate has been perpetuated by film and television for decades.

From Sherlock Holmes to Lieutenant Columbo to Detective Gene Hunt, the sight of the detective lighting up whenever he has a tricky case to think about has become standard fare.

Back in the 1970s, before the regulators tried to curb the amount of smoking on TV, it was commonplace to see chat show guests smoking as they pondered the questions being fired at them by the host.

And while smoking is no longer permitted in that scenario, drama directors still have free rein to show their characters smoking, and they are doing so with increasing regularity.

It's hardly surprising then that many smokers are convinced that smoking helps them concentrate.

What's more, they will point to hard evidence. If they're struggling for a solution to a problem, they find that going and smoking a cigarette helps them to focus on the problem and find a solution to it.

On the face of it, you might put two and two together and conclude that smoking has done something to their brain that helps them to concentrate and releases their creative juices.

But let's examine it more closely. If we can identify what the distractions are, surely we don't need nicotine to remove them.

After all, non-smokers manage perfectly well. And so did you before you became hooked.

In her own words: CHRISTINE, Kent

I got hooked when I was in my teens and I found that smoking really helped me when I was revising for exams. However, I knew I wouldn't be able to smoke in the exams themselves and that really frightened me. I had come to rely on cigarettes to help me concentrate and without them I was convinced I'd fail.

I decided to test myself by going through some past papers without smoking. It was hopeless. I was so nervous I could hardly hold the pen. And I couldn't seem to put together any coherent answers. By the time the exams came round, I had virtually given up on the idea of passing, let alone getting the grades I needed.

Yet when I found myself in that exam room, doing it for real, everything I'd learnt came flooding back. I was amazed. Smoking never even crossed my mind. I passed with flying colours, but for years I couldn't explain what had happened to me. I almost put it down to a miracle.

It was only later in life, when I learnt that nicotine was the cause of the distraction, not the cure, that it all fell into place. In my test exams it was only my own willpower that was forcing me not to smoke, and so I was constantly distracted by the desire for a cigarette. But come the real thing I knew that smoking was not an option, so I was able to put it out of my mind completely. It was that simple.

Most significant of all, I realized that the thing I had come to rely on to help me concentrate was the very thing that was destroying my concentration.

Exercise

It's time to examine what's on your mind. You will need a pen or pencil and a watch or clock with a second hand. Make sure you haven't smoked for some time and don't smoke during the exercise.

Now spend one minute studying the pictures on these pages. After one minute, turn the page.

Without looking back at the previous page, write down as many objects as you can remember in 30 seconds.

....

....

....

....

....

....

....

....

....

....

....

....

....

....

"My husband, daughter, and myself all quit smoking after reading the book. We have been smoke-free for three years. It was so easy, it seems like a miracle. We have NO desire to smoke again. Thank you for making this possible."

L. Formisano, North Carolina, USA

If you found this exercise easy and remembered at least 15 of the 20 objects, congratulations! You've just proved that you can concentrate without smoking.

If you struggled, let's identify what was distracting you. In the form below, write down the thoughts that prevented you from concentrating on memorizing all the objects.

....

....

....

....

....

....

....

If one of the distractions was "I want a cigarette", I suggest you smoke one now.

The reason for encouraging smokers to keep smoking while they read this book is that while you still believe smoking helps you concentrate, you will find it hard to concentrate without smoking. That's because you will be permanently distracted by the desire for a cigarette.

"I no longer look at smokers and wish that I could 'enjoy' a cigarette with them. I look at them and feel sorry for them. I wish I had 100 copies of your book to give to all of my friends and loved ones."
Jarrod, New Orleans, USA

WHAT'S ON A SMOKER'S MIND?

As a smoker, you might believe that smoking helps you to concentrate because you feel less distracted and more able to focus during and just after smoking a cigarette. You've put two and two together and made five. Now look at the situation again.

Before you had the cigarette you were struggling to focus sufficiently to come up with a solution. After you had the cigarette you were less distracted and more able to focus on the problem in hand.

So what really changed? Before you had a cigarette you felt distracted. Once you'd had the cigarette you were no longer distracted? The logical conclusion is obvious. Your desire for a cigarette was what was distracting you.

SMOKING DESTROYS CONCENTRATION

In order to concentrate on something you have to remove any distractions. Smokers are permanently distracted by the desire for nicotine until they light their next cigarette. As soon as you remove that distraction, by lighting a cigarette, you are better able to concentrate.

But you're still less able to concentrate than you would be as a non-smoker.

1. Non-smokers don't have the distraction of nicotine addiction.
2. Smoking only partially relieves the withdrawal pangs.
3. Smoking starves the brain of oxygen.

No wonder smokers find concentration such a big issue!

DEALING WITH EVERYDAY DISTRACTIONS

As a non-smoker you will still find you're distracted from time to time, struggling to concentrate. Thinking that smoking can help will only add to the distractions.

As a non-smoker, you have two choices when it comes to distractions.

1. Do something about it.
2. Put it out of your mind.

If it's a noise or something that's disturbing your concentration, you can either stop the noise or move somewhere you can't hear it. If you don't take any action either way, it will go on irritating you. But if the noise is something you can do nothing about, such as rain on the window, it's easy to put it out of your mind.

As Christine found when she took her A Level exams, if there's no way you can smoke, it's easy to put it out of your mind. When you remove the desire to smoke completely, you will find your concentration levels improve.

CIGARETTES AND BOREDOM

Boredom is having nothing stimulating to occupy your mind. In that situation you have nothing to take your mind off the Little Monster crying for its fix. When you feed the Little Monster, you partially relieve the craving and so you create the illusion of relieving the boredom.

In practice, nicotine causes boredom by removing addicts' ability to occupy themselves with stimulating activities. Such is the state of lethargy that smoking induces. Have you ever smoked a cigarette and thought, "This is fascinating"?

OBSERVE OTHER SMOKERS. DO THEY LOOK STIMULATED, OR DO THEY LOOK BORED AND MISERABLE? SMOKING ISN'T A PARTICULARLY MIND-ABSORBING ACTIVITY

WILLPOWER AND CONCENTRATION

Smokers have been brainwashed to believe that any time they have a mental block there's a simple solution: smoke a cigarette. It's this belief that causes the problem. If you genuinely believe you can't concentrate without a cigarette, then you will find it impossible to do so.

If you quit with the willpower method, you will still believe that smoking aids concentration, so next time you get a mental block you will be further distracted by the thought that a cigarette could help. You'll be tempted to try one cigarette, just to see. And now that your brain isn't being distracted by the thought of smoking, you manage to solve your problem, thus reinforcing the belief that the cigarette helped.

If you resist the temptation, the distraction continues and concentrating becomes impossible. It's part of the ingenuity of the nicotine trap. Whatever you do, smoking emerges the winner. But that's only because you haven't removed the brainwashing that triggers the response "I want a cigarette."

"I haven't missed them. I tried going cold turkey. I tried hypnotism over and over again, but this time I feel completely different. My skin feels better. I feel better. I can breathe better. I can't tell you how it works except that it addresses all the psychological reasons why you smoke. I feel really proud of myself and amazed it's been so easy."

Carol Harrison, actress

ACHIEVING CERTAINTY

REMOVE DOUBT FROM A SMOKER'S MIND AND QUITTING BECOMES EASY

Even chain smokers can abstain for hours if they know there's no chance of being able to smoke.

They can go a whole long-haul flight without a cigarette but not break down into a blubbering wreck. This proves that the problem is not physical but mental. Without the possibility of smoking providing a constant temptation, they can happily put it out of their mind.

If, after you've quit, you get a mental block, just shrug. It happens to us all and remember smoking never cured that kind of situation.

JUST REMIND YOURSELF HOW LUCKY YOU ARE TO BE FREE

Notes

Your Personal Plan

I have read and understood the following points about smoking and concentration:

☐ The belief that smoking aids concentration is part of the myth perpetuated by characters on TV and in the movies

☐ Smoking destroys concentration by making me think, "I want a cigarette." This makes it hard for me to concentrate

☐ Nicotine causes boredom, it doesn't relieve it

☐ If I mistakenly believe I can't concentrate without smoking, I will ensure that I can't

Flight check

☐ **all clear and understood**

Do not tick this box until you are instructed to in Chapter 18.

Chapter Ten

Beware Other Smokers

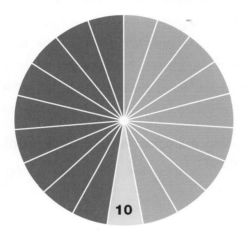

The purpose of this chapter is to make sure you're aware of all the people who might try to influence you back into the trap, because when you're aware of the danger, it's easy to deflect it away.

In Chapter 7 you wrote the names of any Holier Than Thous and Whiners you know and were warned to watch out for ex-smokers who've quit with the willpower method, because they reinforce the myth that smoking provides some genuine pleasure or a crutch, and that you can never be completely free. In fact, you need to watch out for ALL smokers, because it is their influence that has the potential to hook you back in, whether they intend to or not. Think of your first cigarette. Was there somebody who encouraged you to smoke, or was it something you did entirely off your own bat? If it was the latter, what made you think it was a good idea? Don't misunderstand me. You don't have to, and in fact should not, avoid smokers once you're free. Just be aware they may attempt to influence you. When you see through it, it's clear they're just addicts and it's easy to view them with compassion.

In your own words:

ENTER YOUR NAME HERE

You've read other people's accounts of their smoking and how it affected them; now it's time for your story. You don't have to fill two pages. If you want you can just write the key points in note form. What is important is that you think about how you started, how you got hooked and who influenced you along the way. Think of the friends, the relations, the role models, the heroes and heroines.

How does being a smoker and nicotine addict make you feel today?

Did you buy the first cigarette you smoked? Did someone else suggest you have a cigarette?

At this point in your life, did all of your friends smoke?

Who was your hero? Did s/he smoke?

What is the greatest length you've gone to to have a smoke?

Who if anyone encouraged you to smoke in the first place? Who discouraged you?

Does your smoking affect other people in your household? Who? How?

When and why did you make your decision to stop?

PARENTAL INFLUENCE

Most smokers start in their teens, a time when we are all looking for an identity and something to give us confidence. For some people smoking is the safe bet – following the flock, being one of the crowd; for others it's their rebellion, a way to stand out, to show they're different.

We all start smoking for a variety of stupid reasons.

Parents and close relatives are a major influence in their children becoming nicotine addicts. Parents and relatives who smoke seem to be oblivious to the example they set children. They think it's enough to tell them not to smoke: but why should they pay any heed to that when they see their own parents, uncles or aunts doing it?

Did your parents/close relatives smoke?

☐ Yes   ☐ No

Did they forbid you to smoke?

☐ Yes   ☐ No

Did they encourage you to smoke?

☐ Yes   ☐ No

Did they warn you about the deadly effects of smoking?

☐ Yes   ☐ No

Did they warn you that you'd get "hooked"?

☐ Yes   ☐ No

Did they explain to you how the nicotine trap works?

☐ Yes   ☐ No

If you answered yes to any but the last of these questions, it's safe to say your parents or close relatives played a part in you becoming a smoker.

PEER PRESSURE

But it's rare for a parent to be the one who consciously supplies that first cigarette. That role usually falls to a friend – not always a close friend but a friend who makes you feel like you should go along with it. It could be someone you admire, or fear even. You don't want to suffer their ridicule or lose face, so you take their offer of a cigarette.

ROLE MODELS

More subtle is the influence of role models, particularly fictional characters. Throughout the 20th century, if an author or screenwriter wanted a character to come across as cool, commanding, interesting, maverick and strong, a commonly used device was to write them as a smoker. From Sigourney Weaver to Leonardo DiCaprio, the image of a movie star with a cigarette in hand has encouraged countless people to start smoking.

During the 1990s, as the world became more aware of the dangers of smoking, Hollywood made an attempt to cut down, and the incidence of smoking in films dropped significantly from the days of Humphrey Bogart, James Dean and Audrey Hepburn. But today Hollywood is hooked again, with the number of smoking scenes matching the 1950s. This is no accident. The tobacco industry has incredible influence and deep pockets.

The number of smokers in America has halved over the last 50 years, so it's hardly a case of art imitating life – more a case of art trying to influence life?

"I started smoking at the age of 12. Now I'm 29 and I'm a free human being again. I always thought I was lost but I wasn't. Thank you for my life. I mean it. THANK YOU THANK YOU THANK YOU... "

Miroslav Kanurecka, Slovakia

The bulk of our knowledge, beliefs and actions are a direct result of information communicated to us from many different sources. It's perfectly understandable that we should conclude, "I know smoking's bad for me but I can't be that stupid to do it; look at all these strong-willed, intelligent, successful people who smoke. It must be doing something for them."

> **From 1964 to 2014, the proportion of adult smokers in the US declined from 42% to 18%.**

THE PRO-SMOKING MOVEMENT

Then there are those smokers who actively campaign for the right to poison themselves and for other people to do the same by taking nicotine in whatever form they see fit. Their argument breaks down to two main points.

1. Anecdotal evidence
2. Personal freedom

These people don't even work for tobacco companies, yet they do a sterling job of marketing their products for them. They will cite examples of smokers who have lived to a ripe old age on 40 a day, and non-smokers who have died of lung cancer at 50. The implication is that smoking is actually good for you!

And the sad thing is that a lot of intelligent, logical people are taken in by the evidence of one exception, in preference to statistics based on hundreds of thousands that show smoking to be the world's biggest killer.

Those who hide from the health argument are heartened by the second point: that everybody is free to enjoy doing whatever they want, provided it is not illegal. It's a rousing point, tapping into our sense of personal freedom and wilful resistance to being nannied by the State.

But it overlooks two fundamental truths:

1. **Smokers have no freedom.** They do not choose to smoke; they have no control over their smoking – they are addicts.
2. **Nobody enjoys smoking.** They only think they do because they're drug addicts and miserable when they're not allowed to smoke.

CRISIS POINT

It's helpful to recognize the influence of other smokers because they don't only influence us in becoming smokers in the first place, they can also attempt to lure us back into the trap after we've quit.

It's also helpful to be aware of the danger situations that might trigger a return to the trap. The most vulnerable time is when you suffer a crisis in your life, such as a car crash, a bereavement, losing your job or breaking up with a partner. When these things happen you will often find a smoker on hand, offering comfort and a cigarette.

Why do they offer the cigarette? The comfort would be enough. But smokers take their own comfort in seeing an ex-smoker fall back into the trap. It makes them feel better about failing to escape.

That is not to say it's a conscious, malevolent act on the part of the smoker to lure you back into addiction; they will genuinely believe they are doing you a favour because their perception has been turned on its head by addiction.

> *"I was a pack-a-day smoker for over 20 years. I have just hit the six-month mark as a nonsmoker. There are no words to thank you enough. I am buying copies for every smoker I know."*
>
> Juli Goldych, Florida, USA

Be prepared for the influence of other smokers and ex-smokers who quit with the willpower method and start by reminding yourself of one thing:

ALL SMOKERS LIE

They lie to themselves and to others because they have to. That's the only way they can carry on with all the filth, the coughing and wheezing, the slavery and the humiliation. They have to convince themselves that they are getting some benefit from it. And so they end up believing their own lies and the lies of other smokers.

One of the great pleasures of becoming a non-smoker again is no longer having to lie. The sense of freedom is wonderful. While smokers will wonder how you can live without "enjoying a smoke", you know that no smoker ever enjoys a smoke, but you genuinely enjoy not smoking every day of your life – the absolute joy of escape to freedom.

It's tragic to see someone who once appeared so confident and in control reduced to a miserable, defeated shell by the ravages of smoking, but it has happened to enough celebrities – and you probably personally know people who have been destroyed by the effects of smoking. Deep inside, you know that they weren't smoking because it was cool or glamorous but because they were conned, just as you were, and that smoking, far from giving them their character and charisma, destroyed it.

ALL DRUG ADDICTS LIE

"24 years of thinking I had to smoke has disappeared and the illusion is gone. I am a non-smoker!! I'm definitely putting this book in my husband's hands."

Michelle, Lubbock, Texas

> *As smoking declines among the non-Hispanic white population [in the US], tobacco companies have targeted both non-Hispanic blacks and Hispanics with intensive merchandizing, which includes advertising in media targeted to those communities and sponsorship of civic groups and athletic, cultural, and entertainment events. In 2012, cigarette promotion in the USA by the tobacco companies totalled $9.6 billion. [£6.2bn]. (Source: Centers for Disease Control and Prevention)*

Remember, once you've seen through an illusion you can't be fooled by it again. The truth is incontestable.

SMOKING DOES NOT ALLEVIATE A CRISIS, IT MAKES IT WORSE

Notes

Your Personal Plan

I have read and understood the following points about the influence of other smokers:

❑ Anyone who perpetuates the myth that smoking provides some kind of pleasure or a crutch is mistaken

❑ Smokers have no freedom. They do not choose to smoke; the fact is that they have no control over their smoking

❑ Nobody enjoys smoking. They only think they do because they're drug addicts and miserable when they're not allowed to smoke

❑ Smoking does not alleviate a crisis, it makes it worse. Much worse!

❑ Other smokers want me to smoke for their comfort, not mine

Flight check

❑ **all clear and understood**

Do not tick this box until you are instructed to in Chapter 18.

Chapter Eleven
Avoid Substitutes

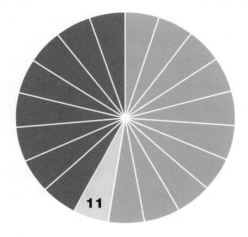

Many smokers believe it will be easier for them to quit if they can find a substitute that gives them their nicotine fix while they get out of the "habit". This shows a complete misunderstanding of the trap they are in. The truth is, substitutes make it harder to quit.

As more and more governments have made it illegal to smoke in public places, the tobacco industry has turned its attention to smoke-free alternatives. E-cigarettes and vaping are all the rage at the moment, giving smokers something they can suck on like a cigarette and get nicotine from like a cigarette.

Smokers think they're getting the best of both worlds: they can feed their nicotine addiction without worrying that they're killing themselves. What they don't realize is that e-cigarettes are keeping them in the trap – still a slave to nicotine and always just one slip away from becoming a smoker again. Most vapers continue to smoke anyway even if they cut down – the result is still fatal.

OTHER NICOTINE PRODUCTS

There have always been alternative ways to feed nicotine addiction, aside from smoking. Up until Victorian times, snuff was very popular. You simply snorted a load of powdered tobacco up your nose. In the Wild West, chewing tobacco was the favoured method. You've seen those cowboy films in which characters are spitting all the time. If you've ever tried chewing tobacco and you've accidentally swallowed the juice, you'll understand why they keep spitting. It tastes repulsive, even to a seasoned chewer. It's not only disgusting, but also fatal.

A modern take on chewing tobacco, and another popular alternative to smoking, is snus – a little pouch of powdered tobacco, which you place between your lip and gum so the nicotine can seep out into your bloodstream through the thin skin of your gums. It's only available in certain countries.

It doesn't sound very glamorous, does it? But the tobacco industry is pumping vast sums into marketing snus in certain countries, dressing it up in colourful packaging and sweet flavours, making it as convenient as possible for users to take.

Why do you think they're going to such lengths? Are they trying to help smokers quit smoking? Or are they using their ingenuity to get round the smoking bans, increase their profits and allow continued smoking? Their objective is to have you smoke when you're able to, and use these other products when you're not.

NICOTINE ADDICTION ISN'T JUST ONE OF THE HAZARDS OF SMOKING, IT'S THE ONLY REASON PEOPLE KEEP SMOKING

THE SUBSTITUTE THEORY

Doesn't it strike you as odd that doctors trying to help patients to quit smoking prescribe the same treatments as the tobacco industry that's trying to keep everybody hooked? They call it nicotine replacement therapy (NRT). They should call it nicotine maintenance treatment.

The theory states that the hardest thing about quitting smoking is coping with the withdrawal pangs.

So if you can continue to take nicotine via some alternative source while you overcome the other aspects of smoking, you can then reduce your nicotine intake bit by bit until you are completely free.

It sounds simple enough. Yet NRT has been an abject failure. Just like the alternatives peddled by the tobacco industry, the NRT solutions recommended by the medical profession, such as nicotine gum and patches, serve only to keep you hooked on nicotine. And people are using them as an alternative to smoking when they find themselves in situations where they're not allowed to smoke, such as in the office, on a flight or on the train. As soon as smokers are able to smoke, they do.

All nicotine substitutes do is make sure you maintain your regular fix of nicotine and remain firmly in the trap.

Who wants to be hooked on nicotine all their life? It will take years to confirm the long-term harm caused by vaping or the use of nicotine in other forms, but deep down inside all nicotine addicts sense the hourly doses of poison are doing them tremendous harm.

JUNKIES

Most people hate injections. Even the more resolute among us who can watch the needle going in without wincing would never say they actually get pleasure from it. But heroin addicts can't wait for the needle to pierce the skin.

Heroin addicts don't enjoy injecting themselves. It's just a process they go through to get their fix of the drug. Smokers smoke for no other reason than that they are addicted to nicotine. Smoking is the process they go through to get the drug. However, they bury the truth beneath layers of myth so they can pretend that they smoke for all sorts of pleasurable reasons: as a social crutch, to help them concentrate, because they like the taste and smell etc.

Using substitutes doesn't free you from the nicotine trap; it puts you in exactly the same position as a heroin addict. Do you want to spend the rest of your life as a drug addict, getting your fix of nicotine in whatever form you can, be it a patch, gum, gel, e-cigarette, snus or even a pill?

"I owe Allen Carr and I want to inspire anyone reading this who may be on the first day, week, or month of their quit. If the world were ending and I had five minutes to live, and someone offered me a cigarette, I would choose NOT to spend those five minutes coughing and gagging. I don't want it anymore. That's the difference between a quit that lasts and one that doesn't."

Brad, USA

In Chapter One you wrote down your reasons for wanting to quit. We've already established that there are more reasons than health for quitting smoking, and indeed the health scares alone are not enough to make a smoker quit. If they were, one chapter on that subject alone would be enough to cure the world of smoking.

Remind yourself of the other benefits to be gained from quitting:

Money You could save yourself many tens of thousands of pounds (or dollars) over the remainder of your life.

Slavery You will enjoy the feeling of freedom from nicotine addiction.

Concentration Without the negative distraction of nicotine withdrawal and with a healthier brain, your concentration will improve.

Stress Without the added stress of withdrawal from nicotine, you will feel more relaxed and less prone to bad moods and irritability. You'll find it easier to handle stress.

Self-respect Think how proud you'll feel to be free for good and leave behind the filth, smell and degradation. Freedom!

All these benefits depend on you getting free not only from smoking but from nicotine. It is nicotine addiction that makes you spend your money needlessly, feel like a slave, lose concentration, feel stressed and moody, and despise yourself for it.

USING A PRODUCT THAT CUTS OUT THE SMOKE BUT MAINTAINS YOUR SUPPLY OF NICOTINE WILL NOT HELP. IT WILL ONLY KEEP YOU IN THE TRAP

"Someone gave me Allen Carr's book. I found it very useful. It's a great book." Lou Reed, rock star

OUT OF THE FRYING PAN

One of the arguments the medical profession uses to promote nicotine substitutes is that, even if they don't break your nicotine addiction, at least they don't fill you with some of the other harmful poisons associated with smoking. In other words, the best they can offer you is to get you off some of the poisons by keeping you hooked on the rest. But isn't one of your main motivations for reading this book to get free from the slavery of being controlled by nicotine?

TO REMAIN HOOKED ON NICOTINE FOR THE REST OF YOUR LIFE IS A HORRIFIC PROSPECT

WARNING: POISON!

NICOTINE IS A POWERFUL POISON

As long as you remain hooked on nicotine, you will be susceptible to the health risks associated with that poison. And nicotine substitutes deliver a larger dose of the drug than a cigarette: typically between 2mg and 4mg for gum, for example, compared to 1mg per cigarette.

According to David Howard of tobacco firm R.J. Reynolds, "The consumer should be aware of the information available about the potential risks of each tobacco product.

"There are none that are safe and there are none that are without risks."

Regardless of health, in terms of your mental wellbeing and living life free from the slavery of nicotine addiction, substitutes are no alternative at all.

Why bother when you can easily quit smoking and set yourself free from nicotine for life?

FIFTH INSTRUCTION
....
IGNORE ALL ADVICE THAT CONFLICTS WITH EASYWAY

"I have tried every method possible to quit. I could not understand how a book could possibly help. After hearing of the success of others I ordered [Allen Carr's] book. I read the book in two days and had my last cigarette that night."

Kat, Colorado, USA

Smokers who try to quit by using nicotine products nearly always end up smoking again. The reason is simple:

THEY NEVER REMOVE THE DESIRE TO SMOKE

The desire comes from the Little Monster crying out for its nicotine fix and the Big Monster interpreting the cries as "I want a cigarette". As long as you keep the Big Monster alive you will always be vulnerable to the temptation of cigarettes.

What happens when you're at a party and you've forgotten your patch, or you've run out of gum, or your e-cigarette runs out of charge or nicotine?

Somebody offers you a cigarette. You think, "Just the one won't hurt." So you take it and before you know it you're back on the cigarettes.

If only there was an alternative that has all the perceived advantages of smoking and none of the disadvantages.

GOOD NEWS! THERE IS!

"I was really impressed. In spite of the success and fame of Allen Carr's Easyway, there were no gimmicks and the professional approach was something a family doctor could respect. I would be happy to give a medical endorsement of the method to anyone."
Dr PM Bray, MB, CHb, MRCGP

There is an alternative that has none of the disadvantages associated with smoking and nicotine addiction:

- ✗ **Ill health**
- ✗ **Mental deterioration**
- ✗ **Expense**
- ✗ **Filth**
- ✗ **Stigma**
- ✗ **Slavery**
- ✗ **Fear**

And all of the perceived advantages:

- ✔ **Relaxation**
- ✔ **Happiness**
- ✔ **Confidence**
- ✔ **Control**
- ✔ **Freedom**

QUIT! IT'S THE ONLY ALTERNATIVE!

That feeling of relaxation you try to achieve each time you light up is what non-smokers feel as a matter of course. Non-smokers don't suffer from the empty, insecure feeling of nicotine withdrawal or the greater aggravation of wanting a cigarette. The only reason you smoke is to try to relieve that feeling.

In other words, the only reason you smoke is to feel like a non-smoker. The only way truly to do that is to become one.

> *"For the past 20 years, I've been sending clients wishing to stop smoking to the clincs run by Britain's internationally renowned quit smoking expert, Allen Carr. Allen has a remarkably high success rate."*
>
> Carole Caplin, fitness adviser to Tony Blair

PHYSICAL OR MENTAL

There is one further flaw in the nicotine-substitute theory. Perhaps you've spotted it.

Nicotine products such as patches, gum and e-cigarettes address only 1 per cent of the smoking problem.

99 PER CENT OF THE PROBLEM IS PSYCHOLOGICAL.

Perhaps you can now see why Allen Carr's Easyway is so much more effective.

The physical pangs of nicotine withdrawal are so slight as to be almost imperceptible and they disappear within a few days. These pangs are the death throes of the Little Monster and when you know they mean an end to your slavery to nicotine, they actually become a source of pleasure.

Killing the Little Monster is easy: simply deny it its fix of nicotine and it will die very quickly.

KILLING THE LITTLE MONSTER IS ONLY HARD IF YOU FAIL TO TACKLE THE BIG MONSTER

The World Health Organization estimates that of the 100 million tobacco-related deaths predicted for the next 20 years 70% will occur in developing countries as tobacco companies shift focus to new markets.

It is the Big Monster that causes you to feel deprived and miserable if you don't have a cigarette. Even if you abstain from smoking long enough to kill the Little Monster, other triggers such as genuine stress can stir the Big Monster into making you think, "I want a cigarette."

You can resist the temptation for so long – some people resist it for the rest of their life, but it is a life of deprivation and misery.

With Allen Carr's Easyway method, you remove the desire to smoke completely.

NON-NICOTINE SUBSTITUTES

Some smokers who attempt to quit with the willpower method try to reward themselves for their sacrifice by turning to other substitutes, such as sweets and chocolate. This is not solving the problem, it is simply moving it.

NEVER USE SUBSTITUTES – EVEN APPARENTLY HARMLESS, CALORIE-FREE ONES

The great evil of all substitutes, whether they contain nicotine or not, is that they perpetuate the illusion that you're making a sacrifice when you quit.

It's easy to confuse hunger with the empty, insecure feeling of nicotine withdrawal. In the first days after quitting, when the Little Monster is dying, you might think you can relieve the feeling by eating. This leads us to the next myth we need to tackle.

QUITTING WILL MAKE ME FAT

Your Personal Plan

I have read and understood the following points about substitutes for smoking:

☐ Nicotine addiction is not one of the hazards of smoking, it is the only reason people continue to smoke

☐ Choosing to remain a nicotine addict is like choosing to wear tight shoes just for the relief of taking them off

☐ Nicotine is a powerful poison. Smokeless alternatives are not safe

☐ FIFTH INSTRUCTION: IGNORE ALL ADVICE THAT CONFLICTS WITH EASYWAY

☐ Substitute-users never remove the desire to smoke

☐ Substitutes perpetuate the illusion that you are making a sacrifice when you stop smoking

☐ Never use substitutes, even calorie-free ones

Flight check

☐ **all clear and understood**

Do not tick this box until you are instructed to in Chapter 18

Chapter Twelve

The Weight Loss Myth

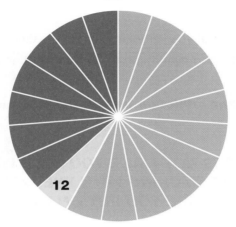

One of the most common misconceptions of the whole smoking myth is that it keeps you thin. This isn't only untrue, it's the opposite of the truth.

Write your current weight here

After you've quit, you can refer back to this and see how your weight is being affected by being a happy non-smoker.

The myth that smoking keeps you thin is supported by images of svelte movie stars and supermodels puffing away on cigarettes. But what about the image of the fat businessman sucking on a cigar? Are we supposed to believe that the smoke from a cigarette keeps you thin while the smoke from a cigar makes you fat?

There are 250 million women smokers in the world today. If present trends continue, this number is set to increase to 340 million by 2020. (Source: WHO)

THE TRUE PICTURE

It's not just cigar smokers who have problems keeping their weight under control. Most cigarette smokers do too, especially heavy smokers. Some people put this down to an addictive personality: just as they can't stop smoking, neither can they stop eating.

There is a connection between smoking and overeating but it has nothing to do with personality and everything to do with nicotine addiction.

Once again nicotine addiction inverts the true picture to create an illusion.

SMOKING DOES NOT MAKE YOU LOSE WEIGHT, BUT TRYING TO QUIT SMOKING WITH THE WRONG METHOD CAN MAKE YOU PUT ON WEIGHT

Many smokers put on weight when they attempt to quit with the willpower method. You probably know people who this has happened to. It may even have happened to you. We've looked at the problem that arises when we allow our intellect to override our instinct and how we confuse the feeling of hunger with the empty feeling of the body withdrawing from nicotine. The two are almost indistinguishable.

As a smoker you wake up in the morning and experience both sensations: a hunger for food and a craving for nicotine. You have gone all night without satisfying either and the urge to do so will be strong.

However, you will not be able to differentiate one feeling from the other. The Big Monster in your brain will interpret both signals as "I want a cigarette".

Exercise

Today, whenever you feel hungry or you're just coming up to a mealtime, make a note of how you feel, both physically and mentally. Common symptoms are feeling twitchy, irritable, unrelaxed, distracted or just a mild, empty, insecure feeling. They are very subtle sensations and if you don't focus on them you can easily not realize they're there. But focus on them and write down what you feel.

....

....

....

....

....

....

....

"I'm forever grateful for that book, it has saved me hundreds of dollars, not to mention all the health benefits. Everyone I know who reads it quits. It's that simple! Thanks again, Allen!!!!"

Craig N, Shelburne, Ontario, Canada

PERMANENT HUNGER

Now compare your notes with the feelings of fear of nicotine withdrawal that you described on page 43. See how the two compare.

Smokers will tend to respond to the empty feeling by lighting up, but what happens when you can't smoke? Because you build up a tolerance to nicotine with each cigarette you smoke, you never get complete relief from the withdrawal pangs.

So a smoker is always feeling something like permanent hunger. The more they smoke, the more frequent those pangs. When they can't smoke they fill the void by eating.

That's why heavy smokers, far from being thin as you would expect if smoking actually helped to keep your weight down, are often grossly overweight.

SMOKERS NEVER ENJOY THAT FEELING OF COMPLETE SATISFACTION AFTER EATING THAT NON-SMOKERS HAVE, SO THEY WILL ALWAYS FEEL INCLINED TO EAT MORE

Satisfying hunger is how we know when we've eaten enough. It's nature's signal that helps us to keep our weight under control.

If we never feel fully satisfied we will always feel the urge to eat more.

As a non-smoker you will be much more in touch with your body's natural signals and, therefore, more able to keep your weight under control without feeling deprived.

COMFORT EATING

One of the things we tend to do when we feel miserable is eat. We turn to food to cheer ourselves up, and not healthy, nutritious food, but carb-laden, sugary junk food. Everybody feels miserable from time to time and everybody is susceptible to so-called "comfort eating", but non-smokers don't have the added misery of being a slave to nicotine, and so they are less prone to comfort eating than smokers are.

Ex-smokers who quit with the willpower method also suffer a misery that non-smokers don't suffer. They think they are making a sacrifice. Remember the HTTs and Whiners? They feel deprived and self-righteous, so they "reward" themselves with sweets, chocolate, cake and other fattening foods.

It's important to remember that this is what happens when you quit with the willpower method – not with Easyway.

WHEN YOU QUIT WITH EASYWAY THERE IS NO FEELING OF DEPRIVATION, AND SO YOU DON'T FEEL THE NEED TO REPLACE CIGARETTES WITH ANYTHING

"For seven years I spent a small fortune on cigarettes, putting up with countless anxieties young people shouldn't have to put up with. I thought of myself as a stressed-out, under-confident person who would be miserable without my crutch. Now, thanks to Allen Carr's Easyway, not only have I stopped smoking completely, but I also look forward to each day."

Jack Seymour, Surbiton, UK

THE METABOLIC THEORY

You may have heard that you put on weight when you quit because smoking speeds up your metabolism, the theory being that when you stop smoking your metabolism slows down and you burn fewer calories. Remember, the Big Monster was created thanks in no small part to so-called "expert" theories like this, which give a perspective that is entirely contrary to the evidence.

There are two factors that decide whether or not you become overweight:

1. The amount you eat.
2. The amount you burn off.

Smoking makes you eat more than you need to because it creates a permanent hunger. It also makes you burn off less because it causes low energy levels and poor lung capacity, so exercise becomes difficult and unappealing.

Smokers become apathetic towards exercise because they tend to avoid any activity that prevents them from smoking. The less exercise you do, the more apathetic you become.

Exercise stimulates feel-good hormones, giving you a genuine high. Unlike nicotine, there is no crash after an exercise high. The mental benefit is long-lasting and there is a gentle return to par.

The impact of smoking on metabolic rate is insignificant. Your metabolic rate does slow down but there simply isn't a carlorie- or fat-burning machine inside your body when you smoke. If you've watched the calories burning off as you pedal on an exercise bike, you'll know how much effort is required to burn off significant calories. Smoking simply doesn't do that.

THE APPETITE MYTH

Smoking is not an effective appetite-suppressant. As smokers we think it is. There are several reasons behind this:

Firstly, as already mentioned, when smokers quit with the willpower method they tend to substitute by eating and drinking more. That's why they put on weight. Yet the process seems to confirm the theory that smoking suppresses their appetite. The empty, insecure feeling of nicotine withdrawal feels the same as hunger and so is often mistaken for it. You smoke a cigarette, the feeling of hunger goes and you're fooled into thinking the cigarette relieved your hunger.

Do you know what happens when a non-smoker feels a hunger pang and doesn't eat for a few minutes? Their hunger pang disappears. The same thing happens to smokers whether they have a cigarette or not. But when they light up on these occasions, they give the credit to the cigarette. Again the illusion of appetite suppression is maintained.

Have you ever seen a cigarette brand that markets itself as a "diet cigarette"?

"When used as part of a calorie-controlled diet, these cigarettes help you reduce your weight by suppressing your appetite."

No cigarette brand makes that claim – for one simple reason:

Cigarettes are not an effective appetite-suppressant.

If they were, it would say so on the packet. No one could stop the tobacco companies saying it… if it was true.

ANOMALIES

It is true, of course, that some smokers are thin and some non-smokers are overweight. Does this disprove the theory that smoking gives you permanent hunger and makes you apathetic towards exercise?

Not at all. The point is that smoking and weight control are separate issues.

YOU WON'T CURE A WEIGHT PROBLEM BY SMOKING, NEITHER WILL YOU INDUCE ONE BY QUITTING

However, you are more likely to have a weight problem as a smoker than as a non-smoker. Next time you are around smokers, take a look at their physical appearance. How many would you say are the perfect build and how many are overweight?

As with all the other illusions surrounding smoking, once you look closely and see the truth for what it really is, you can no longer believe the myth that smoking keeps you thin.

Notes

Your Personal Plan

I have read and understood the following points about smoking and weight:

❑ Smoking does not make me lose weight, but trying to quit smoking with the wrong method can make me put on weight

❑ Nicotine creates a permanent feeling similar to hunger

❑ Ex-smokers who feel deprived tend to cheer themselves up by "comfort eating". I won't feel compelled to do that

❑ Exercise makes me feel good physically and mentally

❑ Smoking reduces my capacity for exercise

❑ If cigarettes contained a substance that made me lose weight, the manufacturers would advertise the fact on the packet

Flight check

❑ all clear and understood

Do not tick this box until you are instructed to in Chapter 18.

Chapter Thirteen

All Smokers Are the Same

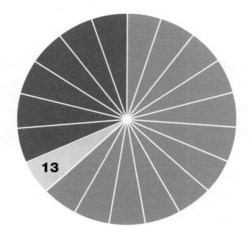

13

Despite the fact that millions of people smoke and millions of people try to quit each year, every smoker has reason to believe that they are a special case. So let's take a closer look at your personal profile.

 What type of smoker are you?

- ❏ Light
- ❏ Casual
- ❏ Occasional
- ❏ Heavy
- ❏ Stopper and starter
- ❏ Secret
- ❏ Male or female?

LIGHT SMOKERS

You've probably heard the old adage, "A little of what you fancy does you good." It means you can have anything you like, even the things they say are bad for you, as long as you don't do it to excess. This might be true for certain things but you have to know where to draw the line. Would you say to a youngster, "Try a little heroin; a little won't hurt you!"?

Ex-smokers who fall back into the trap very rarely say to themselves, "This is hopeless. I'm going back to heavy smoking."

What they usually say is, "I've managed to resist the temptation for this long, surely I can have one and it won't do any harm", or "I'll just smoke a few each day. What harm can that do?"

They couldn't be further from the truth. One cigarette is all it takes to throw you right back into the nicotine trap. And if those smokers knew that cigarette would be the one that would have them continue smoking for the rest of their lives, they would not light it.

It is only thinking of one cigarette rather than 100,000 cigarettes that makes the idea tolerable.

The belief that you can control the amount you smoke is what leads all smokers into the trap in the first place. Does the fly have any control once it lands on the pitcher plant?

It's essential that you keep sight of the simple truth about nicotine addiction:

SMOKING CONTROLS YOU, NOT THE OTHER WAY ROUND

In her own words: MARIAN, Cardiff

My grandma used to smoke one cigarette a day, after her dinner. We used to find it hilarious. If you're going to smoke, why only smoke one a day? I mean, if you like it, surely you could stretch to two. She used to say that that would mean doubling her intake and her expenditure. One was her little treat.

When I became a smoker I began to envy my grandma. Very quickly I was smoking 20 a day and wishing I could cut down. There were certain cigarettes I looked forward to but the rest I had no fondness for. One or two a day seemed like a perfect ration. But I couldn't understand how she managed it. Any time I tried to cut down to even ten a day it drove me up the wall.

One Christmas, my sister and I were talking about grandma's daily cigarette and decided to carry out an experiment. We wanted to see what happened to her if she didn't have her smoke after dinner, so we hid her packet and pretended we hadn't got any of our own. I've never seen anything like it. She spent an hour turning the house upside down looking for her cigarettes and my sister and I were so alarmed that we "pretended" to find them for her, just as she was about to burst into tears!

It was incredible. I had always just assumed that anyone who could get by on one cigarette a day could easily go without. How wrong I was. She was controlled by cigarettes as much as anyone. It was scary.

All smokers envy light smokers – the ones, like Marian's grandma, who manage to restrict their smoking to the odd one or two at certain times of the day. Light smokers reinforce the illusion of pleasure. They appear to be exercising a degree of discernment and choice about when they smoke, creating the impression that it is adding an extra dimension of pleasure to an already pleasurable moment.

But look how grandma reacted when she couldn't find her cigarettes! Do you think she was in control over whether she smoked that one cigarette a day? Absolutely not. When she was unable to get her daily fix, the two monsters drove her to turn the house upside down!

She was as hooked on that one cigarette a day as a heavy smoker is on 60 a day. She spent 23 hours 55 minutes a day waiting for that one cigarette.

No matter how much you smoke, the trap is the same.

NO SMOKER IS IN CONTROL

THERE IS NO PLEASURE IN ANY CIGARETTE. IT'S LIKE PUTTING ON TIGHT SHOES FOR THE RELIEF OF TAKING THEM OFF

NO SMOKER IS HAPPY THAT THEY SMOKE

THE NEXT CIGARETTE COULD BE THE ONE THAT TRIGGERS CANCER IN YOUR LUNGS

CASUAL SMOKERS

Even more envied than light smokers are casual smokers – the ones who smoke every now and then, seemingly whenever the mood takes them. They can go for days without a cigarette, but when they're out socializing they'll take a cigarette and join in the banter among the smokers.

Perhaps you believe this is the ideal way to be: not having to cut smoking out of your life completely but not being hooked for life either – a happy medium. If that is the case, answer this simple question:

WHY ARE YOU NOT ONE ALREADY?

If you claim to be one, why are you reading this book?

PROPOSITION

If there was a book that claimed to be able to fix it for you to smoke just one cigarette a day, would you go for it?

☐ Yes   ☐ No

Better still, suppose you could reduce your smoking so you smoked only when you wanted to? Would that be attractive to you?

☐ Yes   ☐ No

But that's exactly what you do already. Has anyone ever held a gun to your head and forced you to smoke? You've lit every cigarette you've ever smoked – no one forced you.

So you want to reduce your smoking to just one cigarette a day? OK, then go ahead. What's stopping you?

In fact, if that's your ideal, why haven't you always smoked just one a day? Could it be that you would not have been happy smoking just one a day? Of course you wouldn't. Nor is any other smoker.

We all know smokers who can restrict the amount they smoke, like grandma with her one cigarette a day, but can you believe that any of them are really happy restricting themselves every day for their entire smoking lives? Would you be?

As you saw in Chapter 5,

THE TENDENCY IS TO SMOKE MORE, NOT LESS

There are many factors that restrict the amount you smoke: you may spend time in places where smoking is forbidden; you may not be able to afford to smoke more; your body may not be able to cope with any more poisoning; you may be trying to cut down, etc. All these factors prevent you from smoking whenever you want to. Remove them and most smokers would become heavy smokers very quickly.

Now go back to page 161 and if you wrote any figure other than 0, change it now.

BE CLEAR THAT THERE IS NO SUCH THING AS "JUST ONE CIGARETTE"

If you're still envying casual smokers, let's take a look at some examples. And remember two things:

ALL SMOKERS REGRET EVER HAVING STARTED

ALL SMOKERS LIE, TO THEMSELVES AS WELL AS TO OTHERS

Allen Carr's Casebook

#1 THE DYING MAN

A man once rang me up late at night and opened the conversation with, "Mr Carr, I want to stop smoking before I die." He was being serious. There was clearly something wrong with his voice. He explained that he had already lost his legs through smoking, now had cancer of the throat, and had been told that he had to stop or he would be dead within a few months.

He said he couldn't go "cold turkey" so he was cutting down gradually. He had gone from 40 to five roll-ups a day but couldn't cut down any further.

I said, "You are doing the worst possible thing by trying to cut down. Smoke whenever you want for a few days and then come and see me."

He began to cry. He explained that it had taken him a year of tremendous willpower and misery to get down from 40 to five and it had left him a broken man. I agreed to see him the next day.

Remember, fear keeps smokers hooked and when they've already crippled themselves, they're even more frightened. Cutting down makes you feel more uptight because you have to wait for a smoke, and it increases the illusion of pleasure by making each cigarette seem more precious.

This all serves to increase the panic and fear, which is one of the great barriers to communication.

I didn't manage to get through to him in the first session; it was obvious that all he could think about was the fact that he had to stop or it would kill him. But during the second session he managed to open his mind, understand the trap and get free.

One of the key points for him was the joy of no longer being controlled by the drug. When he was on 40 a day, he was hardly even conscious of smoking them, but on five a day his entire life was dominated by cigarettes.

Prior to seeking my assistance, he had been to see his doctor, whose advice was, "You've got to stop. It's killing you."

"I know," he said. "That's why I'm asking for your help."

The doctor had prescribed a chewing gum containing the very drug he was so desperate to kick.

Smokers generally offer two responses to this story:

1. It's an exceptional case.
2. I would never let that happen to me.

Don't kid yourself. Hundreds of thousands of smokers find themselves in this condition every year.

Not one of them thought it would happen to them.

Nobody knew that man was unhappy on five a day. They congratulated him on his achievement in cutting down and he accepted the plaudits. To conceal his feelings of stupidity, he didn't cry in public but put on a brave face. He lied.

If only all smokers would take their head out of the sand and admit their hatred of smoking, it would be finished in no time. It's only the illusion that everyone else is enjoying it that makes it difficult to stop.

Allen Carr's Casebook

#2 THE GUILTY SOLICITOR

A lady solicitor rang up to ask for a private session. I explained that group sessions were just as effective and not nearly as expensive. However, she insisted on an individual session and was happy to pay the fee. You might think, what's so unusual about that? Just this: that lady had been smoking for 12 years, during which time she had smoked no more than two cigarettes a day.

Most smokers would think that being able to smoke two a day is the dream. This is part of the myth. We assume casual smokers are in control. This lady's parents had died from lung cancer before she started smoking and she had had a great fear of smoking before she got hooked. She had vowed never to smoke more than two a day.

Now she was terrified of continuing to smoke in case she contracted lung cancer. But the less she smoked, the less likelihood there was of illness, and the more precious her little crutch appeared to her. So the incentive to quit was diminished by rationing herself to just two a day.

The nicotine trap has many subtleties: the more you consume, the more you want to consume; the less you consume, the more you want to consume. It's like tying someone up so that the slightest movement tightens the rope around their neck.

Do you envy this lady for only smoking two cigarettes a day? Was she a happy light smoker? Of course not. Like the dying man, she was living a nightmare.

For 12 years she craved nicotine but her fear of contracting lung cancer gave her the immense willpower needed to resist the craving for all but 20 minutes each day. She hated being a smoker. While other smokers envied her apparently relaxed approach to cigarettes, she was constantly battling her addiction.

DID YOU HEAR THE ONE ABOUT THE MAN WHO TRIED TO CUT DOWN?

Smoker 1 vowed to reduce his smoking and decided he would succeed by cutting out the routine cigarettes and only smoking when he had a drink. He became an alcoholic!

Smoker 2 was a logical sort of chap and he figured that if he stopped buying himself cigarettes he would inevitably become a non-smoker. He had heard of several people who had tried this method and failed but he was sure he knew why: they felt guilty about accepting freebies from other smokers so they ended up buying their own again. So he warned all the smokers he knew that he would accept any cigarettes they offered him without any sense of obligation to reciprocate. This, he thought, would dissuade them from offering.

Instead, every smoker he knew started offering him cigarettes. It's typical of drug addiction: when other addicts see you're trying to escape they do everything they can to keep you in the trap. With them.

Smoker 3 tried a similar ploy, only accepting cigarettes from his secretary. He developed a schizophrenic attitude towards her: half of him hated her for supplying the drug, the other half loved her for being his lifeline.

But he felt guilty about taking her precious cigarettes, so he started buying her a pack a day of her favourite brand. After three months he was buying her three packs a day and accepting two back!

Smoker 4 decided to cut down from 20 a day to strictly one an hour. As he was only awake for 16 hours a day and could happily spend the last couple of hours before bed without smoking, he figured this was an easy way to get down to 14 a day and he would still have something to look forward to every hour.

He soon turned into a permanent clock-watcher. Every minute of his life became a torturous wait for the clock to tick round to the top of the hour.

He was disciplined – he never lit up until the minute hand reached the 12, but he would always be ready with the cigarette in his lips and his thumb on the lighter.

Restricting the amount you smoke increases the value you place on each cigarette and makes it harder and less appealing to quit. It creates misery and doesn't work.

We try to cut down in an attempt to reach that illusional nirvana between being a lifelong nicotine slave and becoming a non-smoker. All smokers wish they smoked less but they're afraid of quitting completely.

GET RID OF THE FEAR AND QUITTING BECOMES EASY

IS IT WORTH IT?

Light smokers and casual smokers are all fighting the addictive urge to smoke more. They only give the impression of being in control because they don't want everyone to see the misery they endure in restricting the amount they smoke.

But what about those occasional smokers who really can take it or leave it and might go several months between smokes? Surely they're not suffering.

Maybe not, but why do they bother smoking at all? What's the point? Do they think they're gaining some genuine pleasure or crutch from smoking those occasional cigarettes? If so, why wait so long in between? Who wants to wait a year, a month or even a day for a genuine pleasure?

If you envy casual smokers, remember it's the amount they don't smoke that you envy, not the amount they do.

If you like the idea of only feeling the desire for a cigarette on rare occasions, imagine how nice it feels to never feel that desire at all.

Casual smokers, like all smokers who try to cut down, are creating a number of problems for themselves:

1. They keep themselves physically addicted to nicotine. This keeps their brains craving cigarettes.
2. They wish their lives away waiting for the next fix.
3. Instead of smoking all the time, they force themselves to experience continual feelings of deprivation and are always restless.
4. They reinforce the illusion that smoking is enjoyable or beneficial.

HEAVY SMOKERS

For heavy smokers there is no longer even any illusion of pleasure. They know they're killing themselves, they're aware of their permanent cough, the wheezing, the shortness of breath after walking up a short flight of steps. They smoke almost unconsciously. They don't even pretend to enjoy the taste or the smell. They're completely immune to both.

But heavy smokers do still regard the cigarette as a crutch and are frightened by the thought of life without smoking. They are the long-term prisoners for whom release is a terrifying prospect. For them the tug-of-war is particularly fierce. On one side is the fear of life without cigarettes, on the other is the fear that each cigarette could be the one that kills them.

How do they cope? By burying their heads in the sand. Even when they've lost their legs, they can blind themselves to the horror of what smoking is doing to them physically. Anything to avoid the fear of life without smoking.

Heavy smokers are often the easiest to cure. Because of the force of the tug-of-war, as soon as you convince them to take their head out of the sand and remove the fear of success, they're home and dry.

> ★ *The tendency for all smokers is to become heavy smokers. It is only by depriving themselves that not all smokers do.*

> ★ *Smokers think they're weak-willed and stupid because they haven't quit. In fact they're as strong-willed and intelligent as the rest of society and successful quitting has nothing to do with willpower.*

STOPPERS AND STARTERS

Heavy smokers envy casual smokers because they look like they are in control of their smoking. Heavy smokers are under no illusion that smoking controls them, but when they see someone who apparently can choose to smoke when the mood takes them, they assume that person could also stop whenever they wanted. Remember:

ALL SMOKERS WISH THEY COULD STOP

Heavy smokers don't realize that casual smokers are in exactly the same trap as they are.

The same goes for stoppers and starters. A bit like casual smokers, stoppers and starters appear to have the best of both worlds: they become smokers whenever they want and they quit whenever they want. This assumes that they are in control, but as we know:

SMOKING CONTROLS THE SMOKER, NOT THE OTHER WAY ROUND

The fact is, stoppers and starters have the worst of both worlds. They can neither smoke whenever they want to, nor do they have the joy of being free.

The simple definition of a stopper and starter is a poor fool who keeps trying to get out of the trap and keeps falling back in. That's how a non-smoker sees them.

However, smokers do not perceive them that way. Because they think they get some form of pleasure or a crutch from smoking, other smokers perceive stoppers and starters as lucky people who have the ability to smoke, often heavily, when they want and then stop when they want. Of course, the stoppers and starters themselves are only too happy to go along with this misconception. They don't want everyone to see them as fools.

If you're a stopper and starter, ask yourself two questions:
1. If you truly enjoy being a smoker, why do you keep stopping?
2. Having stopped, why do you change your mind and become a smoker again?

The answers are obvious.
1. You don't enjoy being a smoker.
2. You don't enjoy being a non-smoker.

What a tragedy! Neither happy as a smoker nor happy as a non-smoker. The worst of all worlds. Luckily for them, this method works for stoppers and starters too.

There is absolutely no reason to envy stoppers and starters. When they're smokers, they envy non-smokers. They go through the trauma of stopping with the willpower method but never become happy non-smokers. Now they envy smokers, so they start smoking again. Back on the hook, they remember why they wanted to become non-smokers. They're never happy.

To become a happy non-smoker for the rest of your life you need to achieve the right frame of mind. If you believe you're "giving up" something, you might find the willpower never to smoke again but you will always feel deprived. For the vast majority of ex-smokers the willpower eventually gives out and they become smokers again.

Everyone who has tried to quit and ended up smoking again knows what it's like to be a stopper and starter. There's a feeling of having let yourself down and let your loved ones down too. Stoppers and starters feel this way all the time.

If you quit but still regard one puff on a cigarette as a pleasure or a crutch, you will remain vulnerable for the rest of your life. If you want one cigarette, what will stop you from wanting another and another and another?

THERE IS NO SUCH THING AS JUST ONE CIGARETTE

NO SAFETY NET

You may think, "If Allen Carr's Easyway makes it easy to quit, what possible danger can there be in smoking the occasional cigarette? Even if I do get hooked again, I can use the method to quit again."

If you feel a need or desire to have just one puff of a cigarette, then you haven't understood the method.

Easyway makes it easy to quit because it removes your desire to smoke completely. If you have just one cigarette the nicotine trap will get you and you'll want more and more, like the fly on the pitcher plant.

Easyway will set you free. But remember, for the time being, carry on smoking and carry on reading.

"I stopped smoking. I read this book by Allen Carr. Everyone who reads this book stops smoking!"

Ellen DeGeneres

SECRET SMOKERS

Now we come to the most miserable smokers of all. All smokers lie to themselves and to other people.

It's hard to say which is the worst: watching a smoker in the advanced stages of emphysema and finding yourself subconsciously trying to breathe for them; listening to a smoker who has just had a leg removed and is trying to convince you it had nothing to do with smoking; or hearing a smoker who has just been diagnosed with lung cancer telling you (and themselves) that it was all worth it and they enjoyed every precious cigarette.

They are all tragic and pathetic, but most pathetic of all are the secret smokers, who promise their loved ones that they'll quit but don't and then start lying to cover it up. If you smoke openly, you can at least pretend that you smoke because you choose to. As a secret smoker, you have to admit to yourself that you're a pathetic slave to nicotine. Secret smokers go through life despising themselves. Smoking in alleyways and public toilets, it becomes impossible to think of yourself as anything other than a junkie.

I was brought up to be honest in everything I did, and I was, except when it came to smoking. I became a secret smoker and started lying to all the people who most loved and trusted me. The most pathetic thing of all was that I actually convinced myself that my friends and family believed those lies. It was strange that I did. I completely overlooked the fact that the yellow stains on my fingers, lips and teeth and on my clothes were a dead giveaway.

Smokers lie, not because they're dishonest by nature but because that's what addiction does to you.

In her own words: JANE, Nottingham

When my daughter was seven years old she heard about the dangers of smoking and came to me one day and said, "Mummy, I don't want you to die." I filled up with tears and vowed to her that I would stop smoking.

I summoned up all my willpower, threw away my remaining cigarettes and managed to go a couple of weeks without a cigarette.

I thought I'd done well, so I started allowing myself the occasional cigarette as a little reward at the end of the day, after my daughter had gone to bed.

One night, she was refusing to go to sleep and I was getting irritable with her because I was dying for my cigarette. Eventually she dropped off and I rushed to the kitchen and lit up.

I stood in the back doorway and was just bringing the cigarette to my lips when I heard a little voice behind me say, "You're not smoking, are you, Mummy?"

I jumped a mile, threw the cigarette in the garden and tried to wave the smoke away from my face. It was pathetic – I felt so guilty, like a teenager caught by her parents, but this was me, a grown woman, being caught out by my seven-year-old. I felt so ashamed.

You may have wondered why we didn't define the different categories of smoker on page 158. It's because each smoker makes up his or her own definitions. It makes no difference what type of smoker you are.

ALL SMOKERS ARE IN THE SAME TRAP. THE WAY OUT IS THE SAME FOR ALL

WOMEN SMOKERS

Being a mother is just one of the many pressures women endure in modern life. It's no wonder the number of women who smoke has increased so much. Women smokers used to be very much in the minority, but nowadays they are on a par with the number of men who smoke, and in many countries they outnumber them.

This is partly cultural: in the last few decades women have embraced certain behaviours once associated mainly with men, such as drinking and smoking.

But the tobacco industry has also targeted the female market, by perpetuating the myth that cigarettes are glamorous and sexy, help you to de-stress and keep your weight down.

More women than ever are pursuing high-pressure careers and many of them are coupling busy working lives with the demands of motherhood. The stress on women is greater than ever and the lie that smoking relieves stress has proven particularly successful in getting large numbers of women hooked on nicotine. The tobacco industry has exploited this in many ways.

When it comes to motherhood, this is a particular problem. It's long been known that smoking when pregnant harms the baby and so the pressure on women to quit when they become pregnant is huge. Some are lucky and find that they just lose the desire to smoke naturally, but others who try to quit discover how hard it is to escape the nicotine trap if you don't know how to go about it.

This can lead to an extremely miserable pregnancy. What should be a time of unfettered joy and excitement is tarnished by guilt and fear and a feeling of helplessness. Some women become secret smokers, even lying to the father of the unborn child to cover up their guilt at putting themselves and their baby at risk.

Many doctors advise pregnant mothers to cut down if they can't stop completely. Although this is done with the best of intentions, it actually makes the problem worse.

Instead of being free from nicotine withdrawal after just a few days if they quit, mother and baby are subjected to it for the whole nine months. At the same time the illusion is ingrained in the mother's mind that each cigarette is incredibly precious.

Even if they do manage to stop for the term of the pregnancy, the desire to smoke remains with them and for some women the first thought that enters their mind as soon as the baby is born is, "I can smoke now!" Some admit to having lit up as soon as the cord is cut.

Others hold off for a little longer, but because they quit for the sake of their baby, they have a sense of sacrifice and, with the baby delivered safely, they feel they deserve a reward. Sadly, most mothers who smoked before pregnancy and quit with willpower become smokers again after giving birth. And such is the strength of the brainwashing that some non-smokers also take up smoking when they become a mother, believing it will help them relax and maybe even lose weight.

WHEN YOU QUIT, DO IT FOR YOURSELF

If you quit for someone else you will always feel you've made a sacrifice. If you stop for the selfish reason that you will enjoy life more as a non-smoker, there is no feeling of deprivation or sacrifice and you will be happy to be free.

Who are you stopping for?

DEPRESSION AND SELF-HARM

We receive letters and emails every week from smokers all over the world asking for clarification on certain points. Be reassured that as a result of this correspondence, you have in your hands the most up-to-date and comprehensive version of the written method to date.

Two issues that arise with a small number of smokers that contact us are those relating to acute/chronic depression and self-harm. These are two quite separate issues, nevertheless I am happy to handle them in the same breath. Smokers who live with those conditions are concerned that Easyway may not work for them. Those suffering with severe depression sense that smoking helps them deal with the problem in some way. In fact, it's quite the reverse. Smoking has been proven to cause and exacerbate depression rather than ease it. So please rest assured, if you live with that extremely challenging condition, this method will still work for you. Any belief that smoking helps you deal with your depression is understandable but no different from any smoker who believes, for example, that smoking helps them cope with stress. You can relate to absolutely every part of the method and the way we're fooled into believing that smoking helps us cope with depression is eactly the same as with stress. Go back to page 84 and replace the word "stress" with "depression".

In addition to the above, as far as self-harm is concerned, a smoker might say something to the effect of "I smoke to punish myself, or hurt myself, or because I don't care about myself". If you harbour those beliefs you need to understand that you don't smoke because it harms you; you smoke because you're addicted to nicotine. Self-harm may well have been a motivation when you started smoking, but remember we all started smoking for a variety of phoney and foolish reasons: whether it was to be part of the gang, or the opposite, to go against the flow and rebel; or to try to look tough or sophisticated; or just out of sheer curiosity; or just to show the world that we didn't care. The fact is that the reason we start smoking has no bearing on why we then continue to smoke – nor does it prevent us from stopping.

There are many more effective, efficient, and significant ways that you might be able to self-harm if that is what you wish to do. Smoking is entirely unsatisfactory in that regard since it takes years, sometimes decades, to get what might be described as the "self-harm pay-off". People who want to self-harm do it immediately and painfully. Put simply, self-harm isn't why you smoke.

It might be one of the reasons you lit your first cigarette and it might be an excuse you use to justify the fact that you have carried on smoking or to excuse yourself for your failure to quit. But it simply is not why you smoke. To assert that it is why you smoke implies that you have some kind of choice or control over smoking. If you had any choice over whether you smoke or not, you wouldn't be reading this book. Don't get me wrong. Perhaps in the past when you fell back into smoking after a period of freedom, you did so with an attitude of "So what? I don't care if I live or die!" But at that point you didn't throw yourself off a cliff. In that situation it's no more than a phoney justification for returning to smoking; the real reason for the return to smoking was the belief that smoking does something for you.

The great news is that, given self-harm isn't why you've been smoking, you have no need to swap smoking as a means of hurting yourself for any other self-harming activity once you've quit. People who live with depression and genuine self-harming do so with amazing strength and resilience and deserve our respect and admiration for doing so. The wonderful news is that no matter what highs or lows might befall you once you've quit, I can assure you that the highs will be higher and the lows will be easier to handle.

Your Personal Plan

I have read and understood the following points about different types of smoker:

- ☐ **One cigarette is all it takes to get hooked again**

- ☐ **All smokers are in the same trap. The only way to escape is to stop smoking completely**

- ☐ **Cutting down creates a sense of deprivation and increases the perceived value of the next cigarette**

- ☐ **Casual smokers are only envied for the amount they don't smoke**

- ☐ **Stoppers and starters have the worst of both worlds**

- ☐ **I am quitting for my own personal happiness, not for anyone else**

Flight check

☐ **all clear and understood**

Do not tick this box until you are instructed to in Chapter 18.

Chapter Fourteen

Burning Questions

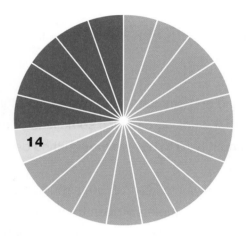

You have come a long way since you first made the decision to pick up this book and end your addiction to nicotine. You have been given five instructions so far and you have absorbed a lot of information. You are well on your way to becoming a happy non-smoker.

You will, no doubt, have several questions that may not have crossed your mind before you began *Your Personal Plan*. These are the questions we get asked most often at our clinics. Tick the ones that you want answers to.

How will I know when I've smoked my final cigarette?

When do I become a non-smoker?

Will I ever be completely free?

Can I enjoy life without cigarettes?

What do I do in a crisis?

Most smokers approach any attempt to quit with a number of misconceptions that they assume to be true. They fear that they will have to go through some terrible trauma. They worry that they may never be able to enjoy or cope with life without smoking.

All smokers wish they could stop, but these fears lead them to put off what they think of as the evil day.

All of us, smokers and non-smokers, are brainwashed throughout our lives into believing that smoking provides some kind of pleasure or crutch. Consequently we find it hard to believe that quitting can be easy.

Your second instruction was to keep an open mind. If you've followed that instruction you should be completely open to the possibility that quitting can be easy. You should also have begun to see through the illusion that smoking gives you some kind of pleasure or crutch.

If you are still unsure about any of this, go back and read through your plan, paying attention to the summaries on the last page of each chapter. It is essential that you understand everything you've read and that you have no doubts in your mind about the marvellous gains you are about to make.

> *Smoking prevalence among British women in 1948 was 41 per cent and remained fairly constant until the early 1970s, peaking at 45 per cent in the mid-1960s. In 2013 it was 17 per cent. (Source: ASH)*

HOW WILL I KNOW WHEN I'VE SMOKED MY FINAL CIGARETTE?

Smokers who quit with the willpower method never lose the belief that they could fall back into the trap. Though they make a big deal of their final cigarette, there is always a sneaking suspicion that this might not actually turn out to be the last cigarette they ever smoke. In some cases they even hope it won't be. If you retain any lingering belief that smoking gives you pleasure or a crutch, the idea of never smoking again will be daunting.

With Easyway you smoke your final cigarette without any doubt in your mind. All desire to smoke is removed. When you stub it out, the joy is overwhelming.

THE FINAL CIGARETTE

To become free from the nicotine trap it is not enough to try or hope that you will succeed. You must be certain. If you're not, you will subject yourself to a lifetime of torture.

When people quit with the willpower method they spend the rest of their life waiting to fail. It is a torture that most ex-smokers cannot withstand and they end up smoking again. For now, carry on smoking and carry on reading.

WHEN DO I BECOME A NON-SMOKER?

Just as smokers suspect that the final cigarette may not actually be the final cigarette, they also assume that they will have to get through some sort of "probation period" before they can truly call themselves non-smokers. This stems from the belief that the withdrawal period is a battle of endurance, fuelled by the knowledge that many smokers fail in the early stages of trying to quit with the willpower method.

> Smokers set themselves different benchmarks for success:
> "When I've managed to go a whole day without a cigarette."
> "When I can go out drinking with my friends without wanting a cigarette."
> "When I can write my monthly report at work without needing a cigarette."
> "When I no longer feel like a smoker."

All these measures assume that the initial period will be hard. Why? There is no painful withdrawal. The only thing that can make it hard is the continuing belief that you are being deprived.

With Easyway there is no sense of deprivation.

You become a happy non-smoker the moment you stub out your final cigarette. You don't need to wait for anything else, just enjoy your newfound freedom. But at some point, a few days or weeks later, you'll experience

THE MOMENT OF REVELATION

It's a wonderful moment at a time when you might normally have smoked when you realize the thought of a cigarette hadn't even crossed your mind. You are free. For some people, the Moment of Revelation passes almost unnoticed. They're too busy enjoying life as a happy non-smoker to stop and think about it.

WILL I EVER BE COMPLETELY FREE?

You may already feel you have removed all desire for a cigarette and you may be impatient to get to the end. If that's the case, congratulations, but please continue reading. There are still pitfalls that even the most eager former smoker can fall into if they're not prepared for them.

You may still have serious doubts. After all, the brainwashing is ingrained and you've been subjected to it all your life. It takes a very open mind to accept that something you've been told since you were a child is actually false.

We've talked about illusions but that panic feeling – topped up with irritability and misery – we suffer (and inflict on others) when we stop with the willpower method is very real.

So although you've accepted that smoking is illogical and you understand how nicotine addiction makes you seek relief in the very thing that's causing you misery, you may still find it hard to envisage your life without cigarettes and so you will be waiting for a day when whatever it was that hooked you in the first place comes and hooks you again.

The fear that "once a smoker, always a smoker" puts many ex-smokers in this position. The answer to the question is yes, of course you can be completely free, but only if you remove all doubt. Some people succeed in removing all need or desire to smoke, yet they still don't believe they're free forever. They think,

IT'S TOO GOOD TO BE TRUE

But isn't life almost too good to be true? After all, birth is a miracle but it happened to you! Believe it. Life is fantastic and it's waiting there for you to live it.

CAN I ENJOY LIFE WITHOUT CIGARETTES?

Think of the reasons why you might ask this question. Write them down here.

....

....

....

....

....

....

....

Now look back at the conclusions you came to in chapters 3, 4 and 5.

If you believe that smoking provides you with a pleasure or crutch, it's natural to assume that not smoking will leave you feeling deprived. For many smokers it's the thought of having to live without those "special cigarettes" that causes the worry.

"The benefits of becoming a happy non-smoker have been endless. The main one is my anxiety levels have decreased to almost zero and my attention span has increased! I'm able to spend more quality time with my son and not be in a constant worry where my cigs and lighter are! Many thanks to Allen Carr's Easyway for getting me back to where I was before I lost my way!"

Gemma, UK

Allen Carr's Casebook

#3 THE DREAMER

This client attended a session at one of the clinics and seemed very happy when he left. He had listened attentively and was genuinely committed to quitting smoking. He was an upbeat sort of person for whom the only real problem in life was his heavy smoking. I thought he would find it easy to quit after just one session.

Nine months later he phoned me up. "Mr Carr," he said, "would you mind if I came back to see you again?" He was convinced he understood the trap completely and, from the conversation we had, so was I. He had gone nine months without a cigarette and obviously was not suffering any physical withdrawal – that goes within a few days; yet he said he had that feeling of "waiting for something to happen". It was a chance remark as we made our farewells that helped me pinpoint the problem.

I mentioned that I would be doing a session in Paris in the spring. He said, "I find it hard to accept that I'll never be able to sit outside a café in Paris in the sunshine, listening to the accordions, with a glass of wine in one hand and a Gauloise in the other, watching the crowds go by." He had just described a situation that many smokers would regard as their perfect setting for their favourite cigarette.

I said, "Think back to the last time you did it; were you actually consciously puffing on that Gauloise thinking, 'This smoke going into my lungs is my idea of heaven'?"

I was astonished by his reply. He told me he had never been to Paris, nor smoked a Gauloise! Such is the power of the brainwashing; it didn't occur to him that he was moping for a myth.

We showed in Chapter 5 that the notion of "special cigarettes" is an illusion, and that rather than giving you pleasure, they only seem special because without them you are miserable and they normally occur after a period of abstinence.

AVOIDING MISERY IS NOT THE SAME AS ACHIEVING HAPPINESS

Over the course of your smoking life you will have had numerous cigarettes that tasted weird, stale or even revolting. But can you remember one cigarette that made you stop and think, "How lucky I am to be a smoker"? You can probably remember meals out or parties when you were utterly miserable because you couldn't smoke, and how relieved you were when you eventually lit up, but that's different.

If you're honest, you'll find the only occasions you're aware of your smoking are when you want a cigarette but can't have one, or when you're smoking but you wish you didn't have to.

IF YOU CONTINUE TO BELIEVE THE BRAINWASHING THAT YOU CAN'T ENJOY CERTAIN SITUATIONS WITHOUT A CIGARETTE, THEN YOU WON'T

You need to analyze these situations to understand why the cigarette appears to enhance them and realize that in reality it does the opposite.

See through the illusion and instead of thinking, "I won't be able to enjoy such and such a situation without a cigarette," remind yourself of the true position:

Isn't it marvellous! I can now enjoy that situation free from the slavery of choking myself to death.

The obvious truth is that all the classic situations that smokers associate with their favourite cigarettes are occasions that non-smokers enjoy too. In fact, they enjoy them more because they are not having to smoke.

Now think of all the situations that non-smokers enjoy but smokers dread.

A holiday flight

A visit to the cinema or theatre

A meal in a fancy restaurant

A scenic train journey

A sporting event

A good day at the office

A hot date with a gorgeous non-smoker

Any situation where you can't smoke becomes a source of misery for smokers. When you become a non-smoker, you rediscover a world of entertainment and opportunities that you can now enjoy, free from the tyranny of smoking. It's the world you used to know before you started smoking. It's called

FREEDOM

If you're still unsure about this point, go back to page 81 and read about "special cigarettes" again.

WHAT DO I DO IN A CRISIS?

OK, so we're agreed that smoking does not give you any pleasure, it only gives the illusion of pleasure by relieving the misery of wanting a cigarette. Does that mean smoking can serve as a crutch in other ways?

We're agreed that cigarettes cause the misery; they don't relieve it. We understand how we are fooled into believing that cigarettes help us cope with stress. We've seen through the con trick. (See diagram on page 84.)

Because of the myth that smoking relieves stress, smokers also believe that smoking helps you to cope in a crisis.

A classic scenario on your TV or cinema screen is the character who receives bad news and sits down to recover with a cigarette. The message is clear: "This character is coping thanks to the cigarette."

In real life, smoking provides no help at all in coping with trauma. In fact, it makes it worse.

Take, for example, the nightmare of your car breaking down in the rain late at night. Even if you've never been in this situation, it's not hard to imagine how you'd feel. You're on the most dangerous part of the road, it's dark and wet and your phone has no signal. No one is stopping to help. Instead they're whizzing by at high speed, splashing you and sounding their horns at you, as if you've chosen to be stuck there in this weather.

A smoker would no doubt light up a cigarette in these circumstances, but the predicament hasn't changed. They're still stranded in the rain. All that's changed is that they've partially relieved a stress that a non-smoker would not have had. They're no less stressed than a non-smoker.

If, after you've quit smoking, you continue to believe that smoking provides a crutch, what happens next time you find yourself in a similar situation? Your first thought will be, "At times like this I would have had a cigarette."

But think back to the last time such a trauma happened in your life. Did the cigarette solve your problem? Or even make it seem less severe? Did you stand there happily thinking, "I'm not bothered that I'm cold, wet, hungry and tired, at least I've got this marvellous cigarette." Or were you still just as miserable? In fact, you were probably panicking about running low on cigarettes!

When ex-smokers who have stopped with the willpower method experience these situations, they start to mope for a cigarette. They don't realize that, far from helping, the cigarette makes matters worse by adding a further stress to the equation.

YOU'RE GOING TO BE A NON-SMOKER, NOT AN EX-SMOKER.

Accept that, smoker or non-smoker, there will be ups and downs in life. If you can do something about them, do it. If you can't, put them out of your mind and move on. Trying to make them go away by smoking is going to have the opposite effect. It will give you more problems. Not having a cigarette but wishing you could will make you miserable – you'll just be moping after an illusion.

Get it clear in your mind:

REMOVING CIGARETTES FROM YOUR LIFE DOES NOT CREATE A VOID

Ex-smokers who don't understand this suffer the misery of turning good days into bad days and making bad days worse.

Addiction versus dependence

So-called experts in drug addiction often use terms that create problems for addicts. The most common is "give up", which implies a sacrifice. Another is "dependence". You are only dependent on something you cannot survive without.

Nobody is ever dependent on nicotine, alcohol, heroin or cocaine – people only think they are. By using the word "dependence", doctors and other so-called experts reinforce the brainwashing and confirm addicts' fears.

The terms "addiction" and "dependence" should not be confused. Type 1 diabetics might be dependent on insulin for survival, but that doesn't make them drug addicts. They have a good reason for using the drug and are in control. Addiction is the opposite. All smokers, no matter how occasionally they smoke, are nicotine addicts: there are no rational reasons for smoking and they are not in control.

BE PREPARED

Because crises and traumatic incidents tend to occur infrequently and without warning, they can catch you by surprise. You might think you understand the trap and have removed all need or desire to smoke; you could go months or even years as a happy non-smoker, but then some crisis arises that throws you off balance and from somewhere in your mind the thought arises, "At times like this I would have had a cigarette."

REMEMBER: thinking something doesn't really mean anything. It's what you do with that thought that really matters.

Instead of saying to yourself, "At times like this I would have had a cigarette," and worrying about it, think how much better you are able to cope now you are no longer a slave to nicotine; these are moments to remind yourself how lucky you are to be free.

GREAT – I'M A NON-SMOKER!

Notes

Your Personal Plan

I have read and understood the following points in answer to my burning questions:

❏ **With Easyway, I will finish my final cigarette with absolute certainty that I will never smoke again**

❏ **I will become a happy non-smoker the moment I stub out my final cigarette**

❏ **Anyone can get free, provided they remove all doubt about their decision to do so**

❏ **Avoiding misery is not the same as achieving happiness**

❏ **Removing cigarettes from my life will not create a void**

Flight check

❏ **all clear and understood**

Do not tick this box until you are instructed to in Chapter 18.

Chapter Fifteen

There is Nothing To Fear

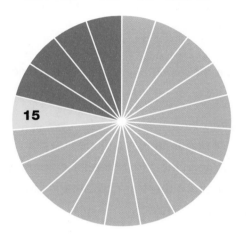

If fear is the foundation of addiction, where does this fear come from? And, more importantly, how do you make it go away?

Make two lists: on one side list the advantages you perceive in smoking; on the other side list the disadvantages.

Advantages of smoking		Disadvantages of smoking	
....	....	....	....
....	....	....	....
....	....	....	....
....	....	....	....
....	....	....	....
....	....	....	....
....	....	....	....

If you've read and understood everything we've covered so far, this should be a very one-sided list. Hopefully you will have nothing in the "advantages" column.

SEEING IS BELIEVING

You are well on your way to seeing the truth about nicotine addiction and understanding the trap. Nothing has changed in reality. The advantages and disadvantages have been the same throughout your smoking life. There never has been a good reason to smoke. There have always been countless good reasons to stop.

There is one force that makes smokers close their minds to the facts:

FEAR

Fear feeds on a lack of understanding. Once you reach the point where you have nothing to write in the "advantages" column, you have nothing to fear. But if you still believe there are advantages to smoking, you will be vulnerable to the fear of success.

The fear of success is what keeps smokers in the trap. They find themselves in a tug-of-war between their fear of the harm that smoking is doing to them and their fear of life without smoking; how will they cope without their "pleasure" or "crutch"?

Because of the brainwashing, they feel certain that life without smoking will be unbearable, combined with the fear of what will happen if they carry on smoking. They end up like rabbits caught in headlights, trapped by fear.

Non-smokers find this impossible to understand. They know that there is nothing to fear in a life without smoking, so they find it baffling that anyone should risk their life by continuing to smoke.

★ *When you become a non-smoker, you will see for certain that there is nothing to fear, only marvellous gains to enjoy.*

NEVER IS FOREVER

Some smokers try to allay their fear of success by telling themselves that they will always have the choice of smoking again if they find life without smoking too painful. "It doesn't have to be final."

True, everyone has the choice to smoke if they want to, but when you have no need or desire to smoke, why would you ever make that choice?

Start off with the attitude that it's not final and the likelihood is that you will fail sooner or later. The only reason you would tell yourself you have the option to smoke again is if you still believe smoking gives you some kind of pleasure or a crutch. If you still believe that then you will always be vulnerable to the temptation to smoke and you will need all your willpower to resist it.

THIS METHOD REMOVES THE TEMPTATION ALTOGETHER

Instead, start off with the certainty that you're going to succeed and you're going to be free forever. Remove all doubt. That certainty is easy to achieve when you remove the fear and panic.

THE FEAR OF STOPPING SMOKING WAS CREATED BY STARTING SMOKING

CIGARETTES CAUSE FEAR – THEY DON'T RELIEVE IT!

"What strikes me most powerfully is that there are none of the withdrawal pangs suffered with other methods. The percentage of success achieved (80%) is extremely high."
Dr Jose Alvarez Salcedo, Head of Medical Services, Transfesa

ACHIEVING CERTAINTY

We have established that in order to quit smoking easily, painlessly and permanently you need to remove all doubt. But how can you be certain that something will not happen? After all, the chances of being struck by a meteorite are infinitesimally small, yet nobody can be certain that it will never happen to them.

As a smoker, you have a considerable advantage over potential meteorite victims.

> ★ *If a meteorite is going to hit you, there is absolutely nothing you can do about it.*

But only you can make yourself smoke again.

Smokers believe they can never be certain that they won't smoke again because they know they don't control their smoking – smoking controls them. Nobody forces them to smoke, but the brainwashing convinces them that they will be happier – or rather less miserable – if they remain a smoker. Any smoker can regain control by removing the brainwashing.

So the only thing that might cause you doubt is your own state of mind.

And that's something you can control. Open your mind, relax and see through the illusions and you will achieve certainty that smoking does absolutely nothing for you whatsoever. Once you have that certainty, you remove all desire for a cigarette. And with all desire removed, being a non-smoker becomes the easiest and most natural thing in the world.

JUST ASK A NON-SMOKER HOW EASY THEY FIND IT NOT TO SMOKE

Of course you don't, because in order for that to happen you would have to pick up a frying pan and start hitting yourself over the head with it, and you can be certain that you have no need or desire to do that!

The same applies to smoking. There is no good reason for lighting a cigarette and sucking its toxic smoke down into your lungs, and once you are convinced of this fact you will have no more need or desire to smoke than you have to hit yourself over the head with a frying pan.

Contrary to what many smokers believe:

YOU CAN BE FREE

In order to achieve this level of certainty you must ensure that three vital points are ingrained in your mind.

1. Cigarettes do absolutely nothing for you.
You must understand why this is so. That way, you will have no feeling of deprivation.

2. You do not need to go through any transitional period.
Forget about any "withdrawal period" before the craving goes completely. Craving is mental, not physical, and yours will be removed by the time you've finished your final cigarette.

3. There is no such thing as "just one cigarette".
See each cigarette for what it is: part of a whole filthy lifetime chain. Don't see one cigarette, see 100,000 cigarettes. See reality.

One of the mistakes people make when they try to quit with the willpower method is they try to put smoking right out of their mind. The result is they end up obsessed by it. It's just how the human mind works. Try to avoid thinking about anything and it will automatically dominate your thoughts.

DON'T THINK ABOUT ELEPHANTS!

What's the first thing that came into your mind?

THE SIXTH INSTRUCTION
DON'T TRY NOT TO THINK ABOUT SMOKING

Notes

GRIEVING FOR NOTHING

For some smokers who quit with the willpower method, the sense of loss feels like bereavement. Throughout their smoking life they regarded the cigarette as a friend, a crutch, or even a part of themselves – something that gave them their identity. They know it's a harmful friend but they still feel a sense of loss when they cut it out of their lives.

We all fear bereavement and we suffer when it happens to us. When we lose someone we love, though we may get over the initial pain, it leaves a void in our lives. There will be occasions when we become acutely aware of their absence: a family gathering, a routine event that we always did with them. It make us feel sad. Ex-smokers who are using all their willpower to stay off cigarettes feel a similar void, which hits them harder on certain occasions.

It's understandable that anyone who has tried to quit with the willpower method and experienced this sense of bereavement will be reluctant to subject themselves to it again.

But what are they grieving for? A "friend" that kept them as a slave, caused them untold misery, took their money and threatened their life. What's more, a "friend" that is not dead but is lying in wait for the moment their willpower gives out, whereupon it will re-enter their life with a vengeance and resume its campaign of havoc and proceed to kill them!

GET IT CLEAR IN YOUR MIND: THE CIGARETTE IS NOT YOUR FRIEND AND NEVER HAS BEEN. IT'S THE WORST ENEMY YOU'VE EVER HAD

Imagine if you lived in a country that was oppressed by an evil tyrant. Every day you lived in fear of your life, you felt like a captive, and every day you wished you didn't have to live under this tyranny. How would you feel if that tyrant was removed from power? Would you grieve? Or would you rejoice?

Q: WHEN WILL THE CRAVING GO?
A: WHENEVER YOU CHOOSE.

The choice is simple:

1. Continue to mistakenly view cigarettes as your friend and wonder when you'll stop missing them. This option will guarantee that you feel miserable, you will continue to crave cigarettes and you will either spend the rest of your life feeling deprived or, more likely, you will start smoking again. ☐

2. Recognize that the cigarette is a tyrant that has kept you in captivity and misery and constantly threatened your life. Seeing it as it really is will enable you to stop craving cigarettes and rejoice in spending the rest of your life free from cigarettes. ☐

If that's a choice you think you're ready to make, tick the option that you prefer.

LITTLE NIGGLES

Imagine if the removal of that tyrant we spoke about involved a few initial inconveniences, such as the occasional power cut, just for a few days. It would be a little irritating but would it stop you celebrating the end of the tyranny?

During the first few days after your final cigarette, the Little Monster will be literally dying for its fix and will be sending messages to your brain that it wants you to interpret as "I want a cigarette". But now you understand what's going on and instead of feeding the Little Monster, you rejoice in its death throes because you know they are part of the end of the tyranny of smoking.

By seeing the positive truth, you don't get uptight because you can't smoke. You accept the feeling for what it is – a slight irritation that's nothing more than what smokers live with all their smoking lives. You recognize that there is no pain and, therefore, no need to panic, and you rejoice in the fact that you are killing the Little Monster.

REACTION TIMES

You might find that there are times, particularly during the first few days, when you forget that you've quit. First thing in the morning is a common time. You're half asleep and you think, "I'll get up and have a cigarette." Then you remember you no longer smoke.

Another occasion might be when you're socializing. You're chatting away and suddenly there's a pack of cigarettes under your nose. You automatically reach for one, then catch yourself.

Such occasions can bring the doubts back into your mind. You thought you'd removed the brainwashing, so why are you instinctively reacting like a smoker?

The mental associations between smoking and social situations, or waking up in the morning etc. can linger on long after the physical withdrawal has ceased. This doesn't mean you're still addicted. So there's no need to panic. Be prepared for these situations and if they do occur, remain calm and instead of thinking, "Oh no! I've been tempted but I can't have one," think, "Isn't this great! I don't need to smoke any more. I'm free!"

A GOOD SIGN

Momentarily forgetting that you no longer smoke is a good sign. It shows that your life is no longer dominated by smoking. Your mind is free and you can return to the happy state you were in before you got hooked.

Your Personal Plan

I have read and understood the following points about the fear of becoming a non-smoker:

❏ If I still mistakenly believe there are advantages to smoking I will be vulnerable to the fear of success

❏ The fear of stopping smoking is irrational. It is caused by starting smoking

❏ I have a choice

❏ I do not need to go through any transitional period

❏ SIXTH INSTRUCTION: DON'T TRY NOT TO THINK ABOUT SMOKING

❏ The cigarette is not my friend and never has been. It's the worst enemy I've ever had

Flight check

❏ **all clear and understood**

Do not tick this box until you are instructed to in Chapter 18.

Chapter Sixteen

Taking Control

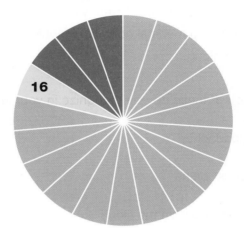

Soon you will be smoking your last-ever cigarette. First we need to gather up everything you've read and understood and use it to unravel any lingering doubts you may have. It's time to take control.

In Chapter 1 you wrote down your reasons for wanting to quit. Remind yourself what they were by writing them out again here, and add any that may have come up since then.

....

....

....

....

....

....

....

....

There are many good reasons smokers give for wanting to quit.

HEALTH

Health is the most common reason. Often without realizing it, smokers live with all sorts of debilitating medical conditions, which they pretend have nothing to do with smoking.

Which of these do you recognize in yourself?

☐ Headaches

☐ Chest pains

☐ Liver spots on the skin

☐ Shortness of breath

☐ Spots before the eyes when standing up quickly

☐ Coughing

☐ Wheezing

☐ Dizziness

☐ Lethargy and tiredness

☐ Susceptibility to colds and other ailments

★ *When you quit, your body miraculously fights its way back to health and you realize just how unhealthy you were when you were smoking.*

But it's the knowledge of the life-threatening diseases caused by smoking that most smokers cite as the reason they want to quit. The link between smoking and cancer has been known for decades; it is now clear that a large number of other diseases are caused by smoking.

 Which of these were you aware that smoking contributed to?

- ☐ Lung cancer
- ☐ Heart disease
- ☐ Arteriosclerosis
- ☐ Emphysema
- ☐ Angina
- ☐ Thrombosis
- ☐ Bronchitis
- ☐ Asthma
- ☐ Diabetes
- ☐ Cervical cancer
- ☐ Breast cancer
- ☐ Stroke

Nobody wants to go through life with a death sentence hanging over them and when a health scare comes along – whether for the smoker or someone close to them – it is often the trigger for an attempt to quit.

But the health risks alone are not enough to make us quit. If they were, we could fill this book with statistics designed to shock you into taking your head out of the sand and quitting immediately. But shock tactics don't work.

Smokers naturally close their ears to the horrific statistics. "It won't happen to me." But harder to understand is how a smoker can keep smoking after it has happened to them. For example, after a doctor has told them, "If you don't stop, you will lose your legs."

No doubt you are convinced that, faced with that choice, you would stop immediately. You need to understand why you might not.

Such is the ingenious subtlety of the nicotine trap that the more we fear the debilitating effects that smoking is having on us, the more we feel the need for our little crutch. The smoker who is told he is going to lose his legs is terrified but, because he's addicted, he seeks comfort in the very thing that's killing him.

Eventually the debilitating effects of the addiction and the poisoning drag you down so far, both physically and mentally, that even though you know it's killing you, you become resigned to your fate.

Although they try to block their minds to it, all smokers are aware from the start that they are greatly increasing the risk of contracting life-threatening illnesses. The more the fear and panic take hold, the more they rely on their little crutch.

Smokers know this is illogical but they don't understand why it happens. They feel helpless and pathetic, which in turn leaves them even more in need of their little crutch.

THIS IS HOW ADDICTION CONTROLS US

Although we know it's killing us, it fools us into thinking it's our friend.

DON'T TRY TO USE THE MISERY OF FEELING CONTROLLED BY A DRUG TO MOTIVATE YOU TO STOP SMOKING, BUT RELEASE AND FREEDOM FROM THAT CONTROL ARE BEAUTIFUL THINGS TO ENJOY WHEN YOU ARE FREE!

When a smoker works out how much they spend on cigarettes in a year, or hears that the average amount a 20-a-day smoker gets through in a lifetime is more than £100,000 ($160,000), it is often enough to trigger an attempt to quit. You only need to think of all the things you could do with that money to realize what a wonderful life you could have as a non-smoker.

But money alone is not enough to make us quit. Smokers will always find the money they need to fuel their addiction, even at the expense of the important things in life.

Even when they can't afford to buy their usual quota of cigarettes, they will cut down, or smoke roll-ups, or beg, steal and borrow to make sure they don't go without. It's a pitiful way to live, which adds to the smoker's sense of self-loathing and misery.

THE MORE MISERABLE SMOKERS FEEL, THE MORE THEY FEEL THE NEED FOR THEIR LITTLE CRUTCH

They fully understand the logic in quitting in order to stop burning away money, and the fact that they find themselves incapable of doing so only adds to their lack of self-esteem.

DON'T TRY TO USE MONEY AS MOTIVATION TO QUIT, BUT THE CASH BONANZA WHEN YOU'RE FREE IS SOMETHING WONDERFUL TO ENJOY!

"I stopped with Allen Carr's Easyway to Stop Smoking Seminar. I wanted to feel free, not a slave to nicotine which does not give you any pleasure."

Gianluca Vialli, ex-soccer player

GUILT

Both health and money come into play if you have loved ones putting pressure on you to quit. The thought of how your ill health or death will affect those close to you is terrifying.

No parent wants their child to smoke, but you know that that is almost inevitable if you continue to set the example of smoking.

At our clinics, we have heard from parents who tried to quit for that reason, or because their seven-year-old daughter told them, "I don't want you to die, Mummy."

Yet even an emotional pull as strong as that isn't enough to make smokers quit.

Despite the burning desire to do the right thing by their loved ones, they find themselves lying and sneaking off in secret to continue smoking.

They despise themselves for it and the guilt makes them miserable.

The desire to quit is immense and yet they fail to escape because they don't understand the trap they're in.

DON'T TRY TO USE THE GUILT YOU FEEL TO INSPIRE YOU TO STOP, BUT RELEASE FROM THOSE AWFUL THOUGHTS AND FEELINGS IS LIKE BEAUTIFUL SUNSHINE AND BLUE SKY WHEN YOU ARE FREE!

THE REAL REASON FOR QUITTING

Despite these powerful reasons for quitting, smokers still find excuses to keep smoking. They bury their head in the sand about the money, tell themselves the health horrors won't happen to them, and lie to themselves and their loved ones that they have or will quit... just not yet.

This constant avoidance, denial and lying adds to the smoker's misery. They can't understand why, in the face of so many compelling reasons to quit, they still go to such lengths to keep smoking. They can only conclude that they are ensnared by something they cannot control. And this in itself is the most compelling reason to quit:

TO REGAIN CONTROL OF YOUR LIFE

When you become a non-smoker there are many reasons to rejoice. Knowing that you are living more healthily and have instantly reduced your risk of premature death is a great feeling.

Finding that you have more money to spend on genuine pleasures is uplifting. Being able to look your loved ones in the eye and kiss them without them flinching at the smell is a marvellous sensation.

But best of all is not having to regard yourself as a slave.

Feeling in control of your health, your money, your relationships, your life is wonderful for your confidence and self-esteem.

On the flip side, feeling you have no control over those things is degrading and miserable. But you're often unaware of just how far you've fallen until you quit and escape from the trap.

DEFENSIVE ARGUMENTS

You can tell that smokers feel they're not in control by the way they answer the question "Why do you smoke?"

Their answers are nearly always defensive and negative:

"I haven't noticed it making me unwell." (Health obsession)

"I can afford it." (Money obsession)

"I haven't got any other vices." (Guilt obsession)

It shows that thoughts about health, money and guilt are uppermost in their mind.

Ask someone why they enjoy a genuine pleasure, such as playing football, and they'll enthuse about the team spirit, the physical exercise, the fresh air, the sense of achievement, etc. Ask anyone why they pursue a genuine pleasure and they won't make excuses about money, health or guilt.

Smokers only give these defensive answers because they know there is no good reason for smoking and that they only do it because something is controlling them.

ADDICTION AND FEAR

The fear is caused by brainwashing. When you remove the brainwashing, the fear disappears and you regain control. That is how you escape the trap.

IT'S EASY

Turn back to page 69. Look at the big blue square and remind yourself that this is what smoking does for you: absolutely nothing whatsoever. It doesn't even give you a high.

Make sure you're clear that the illusion of pleasure that a smoker feels is merely the partial, temporary relief of the empty, insecure feeling created by the previous cigarette. Understand that as long as you continue to smoke you will be controlled by this feeling. The only way to rid yourself of it for good is to stop smoking. Permanently.

ALL SMOKERS WANT TO QUIT

A lot of people find it hard to accept this fact. Smokers and non-smokers alike assume there must be some smokers who actually enjoy smoking and are happy to remain smokers for the rest of their lives. But have you ever met one?

Do you know a single smoker who has never tried to quit, or cut down, or switched to vaping or other substitutes, who has never moaned about the amount they spend on smoking or the damage it is doing to their health?

According to surveys, 70 per cent of smokers admit that they want to quit. The other 30 per cent aren't prepared to admit it yet, because admitting it is to admit that you are not in control, and the thing smokers hate most about smoking is knowing they are being controlled.

ALL SMOKERS THINK SHORT TERM

These days, very few smokers have beautiful expensive lighters or cigarette cases. Beautiful, sexy, glamorous men and women, impeccably dressed in the latest designer fashions, light their cigarettes with cheap, green, plastic lighters. They don't want expensive ones because they hope to stop soon!

"A friend quit after reading your book so I decided I'd order one. I smoked while reading the book, nodding my head in agreement with almost every point. Nine months of freedom now and enjoying every minute. The personal freedom is a blessing and the money saved awesome."
Richard, Palm Beach Gardens, Florida, USA

Why do you think all the nicotine alternatives, like e-cigarettes, snus, gum and patches, are so popular when they first come out? Anything that claims to be an effective alternative to smoking is met with a wave of enthusiasm from smokers. Why? Because:

ALL SMOKERS ARE LOOKING FOR AN EASY WAY TO QUIT

The good news is there is an easy way to quit smoking: Allen Carr's Easyway. It has proven successful for millions of people around the world by doing something that every smoker desperately wants:

GIVING YOU BACK CONTROL

The feeling of regaining control, of no longer being a pathetic slave, is the best thing about becoming a non-smoker again. You are about to enjoy that feeling for yourself.

It is the fear that they will have to go through some terrible trauma that dooms most smokers to failure before they even begin to try and quit. This shows the extent to which they are controlled by their addiction to nicotine. It is only the belief that quitting involves a terrible trauma that creates the trauma. It is entirely mental. When you approach quitting without any fear of a trauma, then there is no trauma.

The trauma that smokers fear is created in the mind by addiction.

The Little Monster creates the mildest feeling of emptiness, and that triggers the Big Monster in the mind. The thought process that ensues creates the real physical discomfort, in the same way that a child experiences the same kind of feelings when a favourite toy is taken away from them.

The child wants the toy; it can't have it and reacts with a great GRRRRRRR!!! and unleashes a tidal wave of bad feelings.

But you don't want to smoke, so when you think of cigarettes you won't be thinking, "I want one but can't have one". That's when you'll feel free. Therefore, you won't have that GRRRRR reaction.

TAKE CONTROL

Taking control means changing your mindset to that of a non-smoker, who knows there is nothing to fear from life without nicotine and understands that there is no good reason to smoke.

The reason so many people succeed in quitting with Allen Carr's Easyway is that they open their mind and realize they need not be a slave to nicotine for the rest of their lives.

It's time for you to get the facts completely clear in your mind:

You won't miss smoking.

You will enjoy life more.

You will deal better with stress.

You won't have to go through some terrible trauma to escape.

Therefore, you have nothing to fear.

Your Personal Plan

I have read and understood the following points about taking control:

❑ **Quitting will put me back in control of my life**

❑ **The fear of quitting is caused by smoking**

❑ **I won't miss smoking**

❑ **I will enjoy life more**

❑ **I will deal better with stress**

❑ **I won't have to go through some terrible trauma to escape**

Flight check

❑ **all clear and understood**

Do not tick this box until you are instructed to in Chapter 18.

Chapter Seventeen

Withdrawal

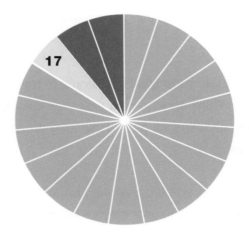

Many smokers reach this stage, completely clear that smoking does nothing for them and that quitting will be a marvellous achievement that gives them back control over their life. But they still believe they have a hurdle to get over: the withdrawal period. Let's dismiss this myth once and for all.

FACT: THE PHYSICAL WITHDRAWAL PANGS FROM NICOTINE ARE SO SLIGHT AS TO BE ALMOST IMPERCEPTIBLE

If this fact is true, why do smokers find it so hard to quit with other methods? The clue lies in the word "physical".

> *"I haven't smoked and I haven't even wanted one. I'm amazing myself here!"*
>
> Joel C, Boston, USA

When you wake up after a night's sleep, your body has been withdrawing from nicotine for several hours (eight if you get a good night's sleep, which most smokers don't).

For the average smoker that's the longest period you go without a cigarette every 24 hours.

So you would expect the withdrawal symptoms to be pretty severe first thing in the morning. Think about it next time you wake up. Are you craving a cigarette? Is there any physical pain? How long do you think you could endure it before lighting up?

Most smokers get out of bed before lighting up; many don't smoke until after breakfast; some even wait until they've left the house for work before they smoke their first cigarette. Not only are they getting by without any physical pain, they're not even aware of any discomfort.

"I read this book by this guy Allen Carr, and the great thing is while you're reading the book you get to smoke. He tells you when to light up. He's like, 'All right, light one now,' and you're like, 'Absolutely!' And you get to smoke all the way through the book. This guy's brilliant. You get to the last page and he says, 'All right, light your last one,' and you're like, 'I don't know if I want it.' By the time you get to the end you're like, 'I don't know if I want to light it, but, OK, if you say so, Allen.' That was it and you put it out and then you're just done. And I haven't smoked since."

Ashton Kutcher, actor

WHY SMOKERS PANIC

Smokers go through withdrawal from nicotine whenever they are not smoking a cigarette, yet they only feel the pangs when they fear they may not be able to feed their addiction. If those pangs were physical pain, like toothache, they would be there all the time and would keep you awake at night.

Many smokers cite the first cigarette of the day as one of their favourites. They look forward to it immensely and if you were audacious enough to snatch it from their lips as they were about to light it, they would not see the funny side. But that's not a reaction to physical pain; it's mental panic triggered by the prospect of being deprived of a pleasure or crutch.

The only time smokers are aware of the withdrawal pangs is when they fear they won't be able to get their fix. With the first cigarette of the day many can wait calmly through showering and dressing, eating breakfast, reading the paper, even catching a train to work, because they have the drug in their possession and they are confident that they will get their fix at the usual time.

Incidentally, don't worry if you do light a cigarette as soon as you wake up. I used to do exactly the same. No doubt you can follow the logic of what I'm saying.

> *"I didn't know what it was like not to smoke. I started at 11 and finally tried Allen Carr's Easyway at the age of 40. I haven't smoked, or wanted to smoke, since. Smoking has become something I used to do. It's not an issue if others want to smoke. I'm finally free. Thank you."*
>
> Victoria Colquhoun, London, UK

STOCKPILING

How many spare packs do you carry?

Have you ever wondered why any smoker needs more than the pack they're smoking?

For any addict, the biggest fear is not being able to get your fix when you need it. The mere thought of this alone is enough to induce panic. Before going out for the night, you check your supply of cigarettes, calculate how many you'll smoke and how many you might give away, and if you don't think you've got enough you will make a priority of buying more before you get to your destination.

MOST SMOKERS START TO PANIC WHEN THEY GET DOWN TO THE LAST FEW CIGARETTES IN THE PACKET, SO THEY TRY TO MAKE SURE THEY HAVE A SPARE PACK, JUST TO AVOID THIS FEELING

Some smokers carry two or three spare packs, just to cover all eventualities.

It's absurd, but these are the lengths smokers go to in order to avoid the panic they feel at the thought of missing out on their fix.

> *"WOW! I never thought I could enjoy quitting. Of course I enjoy being a non-smoker but I always thought the process was miserable before. I woke up this morning with a smile on my face thinking about a cigarette that I did not want!"*
>
> Zane G, Wyoming, USA

THE PANIC-FREE SMOKER

Most smokers nod in recognition at the mention of "that panic feeling" when you fear your supply is running out. But occasionally you get a heavy smoker who looks mystified. This is surprising. If the panic feeling is triggered by the fear of not getting your fix, you would expect heavy smokers to feel it more acutely than anyone. Yet these smokers insist that they don't.

They also look baffled when everyone else agrees that they would smoke camel dung rather than nothing. "No chance!" they protest. "If I couldn't get my own brand, I wouldn't smoke anything."

We've shown that no smoker is in control, that smoking controls the smoker, not the other way round, so how can a heavy smoker possibly claim to be so choosy about the cigarettes they smoke and so calm at the prospect of running out?

The answer is they are not. They only appear to be in control because they never find themselves in the situation where the panic sets in. They've never put their choosiness to the test. How come?

BECAUSE THEY MAKE DAMN SURE OF IT!

The panic-free smoker only remains panic-free by investing tremendous time and money into ensuring they are NEVER low on cigarettes.

Every smoker who is denied cigarettes experiences that panic feeling.

But the cause of the suffering is purely mental. Withdrawal from nicotine causes no physical pain – it's hardly noticeable.

AN EXERCISE IN PAIN

Try squeezing your thigh and digging your nails in, gradually increasing the pressure. Compare this to the feelings you noted when you woke up after a night without smoking. You'll find the pain you can inflict on yourself is far more severe than any physical sensation caused by nicotine withdrawal.

You will also find that you can dig your nails in quite hard and cause quite a severe level of pain without any accompanying fear or panic. That's because you're in control. You know the cause of the pain and you know you can end it whenever you choose.

Now repeat the exercise, but this time try to imagine it wasn't you causing the pain but that it had just appeared and you had no idea of the cause, nor how long it would last. Now imagine that pain being in your chest or head. You would be in an instant state of panic.

The problem is not pain, it's the fear and panic that pain can provoke if you don't understand why you're feeling it or what the consequences might be. The slightest physical feeling that you don't understand can trigger the alarm.

WITHDRAWAL AND WILLPOWER

The myth that stopping smoking means going through some terrible trauma is created by smokers who try to quit with the willpower method. If you have tried to quit with willpower in the past, you'll know how hard it is.

When you try to quit using willpower, you do suffer terrible trauma, but it's not physical pain, it's the build-up of mental panic induced by a slight physical feeling that you can't do anything about. It creates physical feelings, but the real cause is a mental process.

With Easyway you tackle the mental side. All you have to do is unravel the brainwashing and understand that smoking does absolutely nothing for you whatsoever. Then you will see that there is no need to panic. Within a matter of days the Little Monster will die and the slight physical sensation will cease. There is no pain.

Quitting smoking is only hard if the thought of not being able to smoke induces panic. Remove the cause of panic and stopping becomes easy.

THE REAL CAUSE OF PANIC IS THE BIG MONSTER

There are 1.1bn tobacco users in the world, a number which is expected to increase to 1.6bn over the next two decades. (ASH)

"Not only does this book help you quit cold and stay quit, it leads you to taking positive action in other aspects of your life. I truly believe Allen Carr quitters eventually become super-people!"

Evan Beverly, Chicago, USA

Smokers are told that if they can get through the initial withdrawal period then the craving and panic will diminish. But it's not just the Little Monster that triggers the Big Monster.

Long after the nicotine has left your body completely and the Little Monster is dead, other triggers can put smoking in your mind. Social events, mealtimes, a country walk, pressure at work – any situation where you previously would have smoked might put smoking in your mind.

For people who quit with Easyway, this is not a problem. In fact, it's a source of pleasure.

Instead of thinking, "I used to have a cigarette on these occasions," you think, "Isn't it great! I no longer feel the need to smoke."

For people who quit with the willpower method, however, any of these situations can trigger a feeling of deprivation.

That's because the Big Monster is still alive in their mind and it interprets the signals of recognition as "I want a cigarette".

You either deny yourself or you give in and light up. Either way you're left feeling miserable.

In order to kill the Big Monster, you need to get one fact firmly into your mind:

THE EMPTY, INSECURE FEELING OF WANTING A CIGARETTE ISN'T REMOVED BY SMOKING, IT'S CAUSED BY IT

WITHDRAWING WITH CONFIDENCE

We have established that the feeling of withdrawal is so slight that it is barely perceptible. Smokers suffer it throughout their smoking lives without even noticing.

When you smoked your first cigarette you created a Little Monster inside your body, like a tapeworm, that feeds on nicotine. Try to visualize that Little Monster. It's vile, isn't it?

In fact, on the next page, why not draw your impression of what the Little Monster inside you looks like.

Now imagine killing the Little Monster. How are you going to do it? There is only one way: by cutting off its supply of nicotine. As soon as you do, it will begin to die.

It will shrink and shrivel away to nothing.

Imagine it writhing in agony and rejoice in starving it to death. This isn't a cute monster. It's an evil parasite with only one aim – to kill you!

Even if you find the feeling uncomfortable, there is no need to panic. Think about the exercise with pain. How much pain can you withstand without panicking? Remind yourself that this is not a physical pain and you are in control. You know that it will disappear in a few days and so you have nothing to fear.

On the contrary, you have every reason to rejoice. You are destroying a mortal enemy.

THE LITTLE MONSTER

It is essential that you understand three points:

SMOKING DOES ABSOLUTELY NOTHING FOR YOU WHATSOEVER

THE EMPTY, INSECURE FEELING OF WANTING A CIGARETTE IS NOT REMOVED BY SMOKING, IT'S CAUSED BY IT

THE ONLY REASON YOU EVER BELIEVED THE OPPOSITE WAS DUE TO BRAINWASHING AND ADDICTION

"I quit about two years ago with Allen Carr's Easyway and felt so happy and free. I never had any desire to smoke. I never had any sense of withdrawal or of being deprived. I had no problem going out for a drink with friends while they were smoking around me, offering me cigarettes. That had always been my downfall when trying to quit before."

Martin Byrne, Northern Ireland

I'M CURED!

It takes around three to five days for all noticeable signs of physical withdrawal to cease, after which the Little Monster is dead. During this period, smokers who quit with the willpower method tend to find that they are completely obsessed with not being allowed to smoke. They concentrate all their willpower into getting through this period and resisting the temptation to smoke.

Gradually this obsession subsides until, after around three weeks, they suddenly realize that they haven't thought about smoking for a while. It's a thrilling moment. The belief that they will always be miserable without a cigarette is replaced with the belief that time solves the problem.

It's also a dangerous moment. They suddenly feel they have gained control. What harm would it do to celebrate with a cigarette? They know now that they have what it takes to quit.

Oh dear! The trap has got them again. In fact, it never let them go. It was merely toying with them. As long as you believe smoking gives you pleasure or a crutch, you will remain in the trap.

So they smoke just one cigarette. What's the problem? Why can't they just quit again?

"My desire to smoke faded. By the end, I struggled to even light my final cigarette. I'm just not interested in smoking any more."

Rick J, Atlanta, USA

JUST ONE CIGARETTE – WHAT'S THE HARM?

That cigarette might taste unpleasant. It will also give them no illusion of pleasure or a crutch because they are no longer withdrawing from the previous cigarette.

> *Remember, the only reason a smoker believes the cigarette gives them pleasure or a crutch is because it partially relieves the withdrawal from the previous cigarette. For the smoker who has completely withdrawn from nicotine, there is no physical withdrawal to relieve and so there is no illusion of pleasure unless they retain the brainwashing. If they've been moping for a cigarette, that's the only reason they might experience a sense of relief.*

However, they have now put nicotine back into their body, restarting the vicious circle. When the nicotine leaves their body, doubt will creep in. One little voice will be saying, "That tasted awful." Another will be saying, "Maybe, but I want another one."

They will find the willpower to resist smoking again immediately. After all, they want to prove to themselves that they're in control. So they allow what they consider to be a safe period to pass. Now they can say to themselves, "I smoked one before and didn't get hooked, so what's the harm in having another?"

Ring any bells? It's not long before they're smoking as much, if not more, than before they quit.

Smokers who try to quit without destroying the Big Monster are always vulnerable to falling back into the trap. And every time you fall back in, you reinforce the myth that quitting is hard.

ARE YOU READY?

Soon you're going to smoke your final cigarette. If that thought fills you with panic, remember: the tobacco companies depend on that fear and panic to keep you hooked. Also remember: nicotine doesn't relieve fear and panic, it causes them. Compose yourself for a moment. Is there really any reason to panic?

NOTHING BAD CAN HAPPEN BECAUSE YOU STOP SMOKING

Now think of the marvellous gains you will enjoy as a non-smoker.

More money

More energy

More confidence

More self-respect

Why wait? You can start enjoying these things immediately.

> ★ *You have done all the hard work to understand smokers and you now know how to escape.*

You are fully equipped to succeed at something which you never thought possible, something which will impact positively on the length, quality and enjoyment of the rest of your life.

> *Teens exposed to the greatest amount of smoking in movies were 2.6 times more likely to start smoking themselves compared with teens who watched the least amount of smoking in movies.*
> *(Source: www.lung.org)*

Your Personal Plan

I have read and understood the following points about withdrawal:

☐ There is no physical pain

☐ The panic of withdrawal is the fear of missing out on your fix of the drug

☐ Kill the Little Monster and the addiction is dead

☐ Kill the Big Monster and I remove the fear

☐ Nothing bad can happen because I stop smoking

Flight check

☐ all clear and understood

Do not tick this box until you are instructed to in Chapter 18.

Chapter Eighteen
Your Final Cigarette

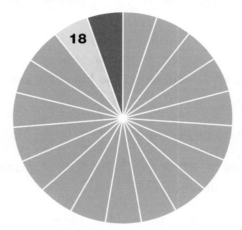

The ritual of the final cigarette is the crowning moment in your escape from the nicotine trap. You should be feeling elated at the marvellous gains you are making, and champing at the bit to get on with enjoying life as a non-smoker.

For any smoker who quits, there has to be a final cigarette. How you approach that cigarette depends on your state of mind. It could either be a terrifying prospect, like the moment you jump to safety from a burning building, or it can be a thrill, like a parachute jump.

For many people who quit with Easyway, the final cigarette is neither a terror nor a thrill. That's because they have already experienced the thrill – they know they no longer have any need or desire to smoke – and they see no need to smoke the final cigarette. If you are one of them, that's great. But unless you haven't smoked for a day or so, it is important that you do go through the ritual of smoking the final cigarette.

Exercise

USE YOUR PERSONAL PLAN

Some smokers reach this stage believing they have understood everything but the nerves of the big occasion make them doubt themselves. This is quite normal. You are about to achieve something wonderful, a genuine high point in your life. It's only natural that you should feel nervous.

However, it's important that your nerves don't lead you to doubt or forget everything you've learned. So whether you are nervous or not take the time now to read through your personal plan at the end of each chapter and remind yourself of everything you know and understand about the nicotine trap.

With each item, ask yourself again:
Do I understand this?
Do I agree with it?
Do I believe it?
Am I following it?

If you have any doubts, re-read the chapter and make sure you can answer those four questions in the affirmative. It's now time for your "Flight Check"; tick the "all clear and understood" box at the end. Once you have ticked the box at the end of every chapter, you are ready for your final cigarette. All you need to do is choose your moment.

"If you or someone you know wants to quit, buy this book. It worked for me and about 20 other people I know. Seriously."

Jason Mraz, singer-songwriter

THE PERFECT TIME TO QUIT

Have you ever watched a child on a high diving board for the first time? They walk up to the edge, look down, begin to take up the correct position, look down again, then back away nervously. Their mum calls them back down but they don't want to come down. They want to dive. They know they can do it and they know they will feel fantastic after they do, but they're nervous.

They walk confidently to the edge of the board again and this time it really looks like they're going to dive. But no, they back away again.

This can go on for several minutes and usually ends up in a rather ungainly example of a dive.

Smokers go through a similar rigmarole. They want to take the plunge but whenever they get close to the brink it never feels like quite the right time.

In order to give themselves that final mental push over the edge, they plan their attempt to quit to coincide with an immoveable deadline.

If you're waiting for the perfect time to quit, remind yourself of the real reason for quitting.

CONTROL

When you wait for a special occasion to trigger your attempt to quit, you are relinquishing control. Take control. Now!!

MEANINGLESS DAYS

Two types of occasion often provide the springboard for an attempt to quit: one is a traumatic event such as a health scare; the other is a special day such as New Year's Day. We refer to them as "meaningless days" because they have no relevance to your smoking, other than to provide a deadline for stopping. There would be nothing wrong with that if it helped, but meaningless days cause more harm than good.

New Year's Day is by far the most popular meaningless day. So many smokers make it a resolution to kick the filthy weed once and for all. Few succeed.

By midnight on New Year's Eve they've smoked so much over the Christmas holiday period that they're literally sick of the taste in their mouths and the congestion in their lungs that they're determined to boot it into touch. But after a few days the toxins have left their body and they're feeling more clear-headed. The Little Monster is still crying out for its fix and because their aversion to smoking has weakened considerably they think, "What's the harm?" and light a cigarette. And another and another.

Meaningless days encourage us to go through the motions of half-hearted attempts to quit, only to suffer a period of deprivation followed by failure that ingrains in our mind how difficult it is to stop. Our willpower is exhausted and it's not until the fear of stopping is outweighed by the desire to stop that we resolve to make another attempt.

ALL SMOKERS WISH THEY COULD QUIT

But we spend our lives as smokers looking for excuses to put off the evil day. Meaningless days merely provide us with an excuse.

CRISIS POINT

Then there are those events we had always assured ourselves would make us quit on the spot, like health scares.

"Oh sure, I smoke, but if a doctor told me 'quit or die', I know exactly what I'd do."

Yet enough smokers have continued to smoke after being told it's killing them to prove that this is false confidence.

When it comes to the crunch, they find they simply don't have the control over their smoking that they thought they had.

They discover that trauma actually makes them feel more in need of what they perceive as their little crutch, rather than giving them the aversion they thought it would, and despite the horrors that they face, they still kid themselves that they're somehow better off as smokers.

If you've left it to a crisis point to make your attempt to quit, take a step back. Remind yourself that health is just part of the reason for quitting and that the biggest gain you make is becoming free from the slavery of nicotine addiction. You're not "giving up" anything for the sake of your health, you're making a positive decision to choose freedom.

Whatever condition your health is in right now, you're better off as a non-smoker.

AWAY FROM IT ALL

Another popular time to try and quit is your annual holiday. The theory is that, away from the pressure of work, you'll be in a stronger state to fight through the trauma of withdrawal.

Can you spot the obvious flaw in this argument?

That's right, there is no trauma of withdrawal. You only feel stressed by withdrawal if you still have a need or desire to smoke.

Other smokers choose a time when all is quiet on the social scene because they think it will mean less chance of getting tempted. But if you've removed the temptation altogether, there is no need to worry about social occasions.

The real problem with both these approaches is that they leave a lingering doubt. If you've deliberately chosen a quiet time to quit, what will happen when things start hotting up again? You can't be sure.

With Easyway, you achieve absolute certainty before you smoke your final cigarette. You are encouraged to go out and handle stress, enjoy meals, drinks and social occasions right from the start. That way you prove to yourself right away that, even during what you feared would be the most difficult times, you're still happy to be free.

THE SEVENTH INSTRUCTION
DON'T WAIT FOR THE RIGHT TIME TO QUIT – DO IT NOW!

That's what you would tell a heroin addict. That's what your loved ones would tell you. There is nothing to gain by waiting. The fact that you've come this far in the book indicates that you understand the nature of the trap and are ready to become a happy non-smoker.

YOUR FINAL CIGARETTE

For some smokers, the excitement of becoming a non-smoker is almost frightening. As you reach for your final cigarette and take it out of the packet, your heartbeat quickens and your hands start to shake.

The thought of quitting for good is almost too good to be true.

Not long ago you believed that it was impossible to quit without immense willpower and having to go through some terrible trauma.

The fact that your mindset has been turned inside out in such a short space of time may lead you to question whether this is really possible.

It's not only possible, it's perfectly natural. More importantly, you've done it!

The only reason you ever thought otherwise was because you had been fed a lot of false information. Let's remind ourselves of the facts.

> ★ *You had no desire to smoke before you started and you have no desire to smoke now.*

> ★ *The empty, insecure feeling of wanting a cigarette is not relieved by smoking, it is caused by it.*

> ★ *Smoking does not aid concentration, it only adds a negative distraction, which is partially relieved by smoking.*

> ★ *Smoking does not relieve stress, it adds to it. The stress of nicotine withdrawal and "wanting" a cigarette is something non-smokers don't suffer.*

★ *There is no such thing as "just the one" cigarette. See reality – see 100,000 cigarettes!*

★ *Being a smoker has nothing to do with your personality or genetic make-up. Anyone can become addicted to nicotine. And anyone can get free.*

★ *Substitutes don't make quitting easier, they make it harder. You don't get free of a drug by taking more of the drug.*

★ *Addiction is 99 per cent mental. The physical withdrawal is so slight as to be almost imperceptible.*

★ *There is no painful withdrawal period. You can get on with enjoying life as a non-smoker the second you stub out your final cigarette with no lingering need or desire to smoke.*

★ *There is no need to avoid thinking about smoking. Whenever the thought enters your head, rejoice. You no longer need to live with that filth and degradation.*

★ *Don't wait to quit. As soon as you achieve the right mindset, with no need or desire to smoke, waste no time in leaving your life of slavery behind.*

Exercise

FINISH THE JOB

Take a cigarette out of the packet. Look at it. Smell it.

Before you bring the final cigarette to your lips, it's important that you are 100 per cent certain about your decision to quit. You should be in a very happy frame of mind. You are about to make one of the most important achievements of your life.

Make all your thoughts positive. Instead of thinking, "I must never smoke again," start thinking, "This is great! I don't ever need to stick these filthy things in my mouth again."

You are about to achieve something you thought was going to be incredibly hard, possibly even beyond you. You have the Big Monster and Little Monster at your mercy. Remember the misery they've caused you and all the reasons you hated being a smoker. Those monsters are your mortal enemies. Show no mercy in destroying them once and for all.

Some smokers reach this point with the Big Monster well and truly dead. They are so convinced that they never want to smoke another cigarette that they ask to skip the ritual of the final cigarette. It's great that they feel that way, but unless you've not smoked for a day or so, the ritual is important for several reasons.

You're curing yourself of a terrible disease and achieving something marvellous, something all smokers would love to achieve, something smokers and non-smokers alike will respect you for.

THE PERSON WHO WILL BE MOST PROUD OF YOU IS YOU

This method makes it easy to quit, but don't underplay the scale of your achievement. It may not take willpower but it does take courage – the courage to open your mind, engage in the process and then go for it.

You become a non-smoker the moment you stub out your final cigarette, so it's important to recognize that moment and make it triumphant. Think:

YIPPEE! I'M A NON-SMOKER. I'M FREE!

Exercise

Now light your final cigarette and take a puff. Look at the filter tip. See that it's already discoloured. As you smoke the cigarette, focus on the vile smell, the disgusting taste, the filth you're putting into your body.

As you near the end of the cigarette, banish any lingering sense of gloom and doom from your mind and embrace the excitement of becoming a non-smoker. And when you're ready to cross the finish line, make a vow never to let nicotine into your body again, breathing it deep into your lungs, take the cigarette from your lips and stub it out with a feeling of triumph. Don't worry if you don't smoke it right down to the butt. That's fine.

CONGRATULATIONS! YOU'RE FREE!

YOU'RE A HAPPY NON-SMOKER

Chapter Nineteen
Life as a Non-Smoker

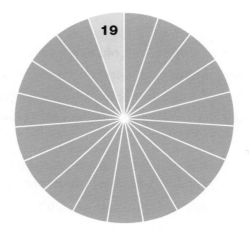

As soon as you stub out your final cigarette you can get on with enjoying life as a non-smoker. You should be feeling great. To ensure that you remain a happy non-smoker for the rest of your life, all you need to do is follow the rest of the instructions.

Don't wait for anything to happen. You're free. You're a non-smoker already.

You are already a non-smoker from the moment you extinguish your final cigarette. You've cut off the supply of nicotine and unlocked the door of your prison, and walked to freedom.

Accept that in life in general there will be good days and bad days. Because you will be stronger both physically and mentally, you'll enjoy the good times more and handle the bad times better.

Be aware that a very important change has happened in your life. It can take time for your mind and body to adjust. Don't worry if you feel different or disorientated for a few days. Just accept it. It's a wonderful feeling of "renewal".

Remember you've stopped smoking, you haven't stopped living. You can now start enjoying life to the full. Don't alter your lifestyle unless there is something you particularly want to change.

Don't avoid smokers or smoking situations.
Go out and enjoy social situations and handle stress right from the start. If you normally take a smoking break at work, carry on taking the break. There's no reason you should miss out on a break if you want one.

Don't envy smokers. They envy you.

When you're with smokers, remember you're not being deprived, they are. They will be envying you because they will be wishing they could be like you: free.

Forget substitutes.
You don't need them and they don't work.

Never doubt or question your decision to quit.
You know it's the right one. If you mope after a cigarette you will put yourself in an impossible position: miserable if you don't have one and even more miserable if you do.

Remember there is no such thing as "just one cigarette".
If the thought enters your mind, make sure you think, "Yippee! I don't have to smoke any more."

Throw away your cigarettes and lighter. Never have cigarettes in your possession. If you do, you open the door to doubt and almost guarantee failure. Would you advise an alcoholic to keep a flask of whisky in his pocket?

It doesn't matter if your partner or flatmate smokes, having their cigarettes around won't cause a problem. It's only a problem if you retain YOUR cigarettes.

Never take nicotine again, in any shape or form.
All forms of nicotine product lead to the same result: addiction. As soon as you let nicotine into your life, it's only a matter of time before you find yourself smoking again.

THE INSTRUCTIONS

Here's a recap of the instructions you've followed throughout the book.

1. FOLLOW ALL THE INSTRUCTIONS (page 21)

2. KEEP AN OPEN MIND (page 40)

3. START OUT WITH A FEELING OF EXCITEMENT AND ELATION (page 48)

4. NEVER DOUBT YOUR DECISION TO QUIT (page 73)

5. IGNORE ALL ADVICE THAT CONFLICTS WITH EASYWAY (page 143)

6. DON'T TRY NOT TO THINK ABOUT SMOKING (page 200)

7. DON'T WAIT FOR THE RIGHT TIME TO QUIT – DO IT NOW! (page 237)

If you've turned straight to this page before reading the rest of the book, in the hope of finding a short-cut solution to your smoking problem, please go back to the beginning and read the book all the way through.

Everybody who has done that reaches this page with the elation of knowing they have quit smoking for good.

If you have any questions or concerns at all, we can help. Just call your local Easyway clinic. They'll be happy to answer any queries you may have.

CONGRATULATIONS ON BEING FREE. PLEASE TELL THE WORLD ABOUT ALLEN CARR'S EASYWAY.

YIPPEE – I'M FREE!

Please use this QR link or the web address to record your video, telling the world you are free and are no longer addicted to nicotine.
http://delivr.com/2c4e7

ALLEN CARR'S EASYWAY CLINICS

The following list indicates the countries where Allen Carr's Easyway To Stop Smoking Clinics are operational at the time of printing. Check www.allencarr.com for latest additions to this list.

The success rate at the clinics, based on the three-month money-back guarantee, is over 90 per cent. Selected clinics also offer sessions that deal with alcohol, other drugs and weight issues. Please check with your nearest clinic, listed on the following pages, for details.

Allen Carr's Easyway guarantees that you will find it easy to stop at the clinics or your money back.

JOIN US!

Allen Carr's Easyway Clinics have spread throughout the world with incredible speed and success. Our global network now covers more than 150 cities in over 50 countries. This amazing growth has been achieved entirely organically. Former addicts, just like you, were so impressed by the ease with which they stopped that they felt inspired to contact us to see how they could bring the method to their region. If you feel the same, contact us for details on how to become an Allen Carr's Easyway To Stop Smoking or an Allen Carr's Easyway To Stop Drinking franchisee.

Email us at: **join-us@allencarr. com** including your full name, postal address and region of interest.

SUPPORT US!

No, don't send us money!

You have achieved something really marvellous. Every time we hear of someone escaping from the sinking ship, we get a feeling of enormous satisfaction.

It would give us great pleasure to hear that you have freed yourself from the slavery of addiction so please visit the following web page where you can tell us of your success, inspire others to follow in your footsteps and hear about ways you can help to spread the word.

www.allencarr.com/444/support-us

You can "like" our Facebook page here

www.facebook.com/AllenCarr

Together, we can help further Allen Carr's mission: to cure the world of addiction.

LONDON CLINIC AND WORLDWIDE HEAD OFFICE

Park House, 14 Pepys Road,
Raynes Park, London SW20 8NH
Tel: +44 (0)20 8944 7761
Fax: +44 (0)20 8944 8619
Email: mail@allencarr.com
Website: www.allencarr.com
Therapists: John Dicey, Colleen Dwyer, Crispin Hay, Emma Hudson, Rob Fielding, Sam Carroll, Sam Bonner

Worldwide Press Office

Contact: John Dicey
Tel: +44 (0)7970 88 44 52
Email: media@allencarr.com

UK Clinic Information and Central Booking Line

Tel: 0800 389 2115

UK CLINICS

Belfast

Tel: 0845 094 3244
Therapist: Tara Evers-Cheung
Email: tara@easywayni.com
Website: www.allencarr.com

Birmingham

Tel & Fax: +44 (0)121 423 1227
Therapists: John Dicey, Colleen Dwyer, Crispin Hay, Rob Fielding, Sam Carroll
Email: info@allencarr.com

Website: www.allencarr.com

Bournemouth

Tel: 0800 028 7257
Therapists: John Dicey, Colleen Dwyer, Emma Hudson, Sam Carroll
Email: info@allencarr.com
Website: www.allencarr.com

Brighton

Tel: 0800 028 7257
Therapists: John Dicey, Colleen Dwyer, Emma Hudson, Sam Carroll
Email: info@allencarr.com
Website: www.allencarr.com

Bristol

Tel: +44 (0)117 950 1441
Therapist: David Key
Email: stop@easywaysouthwest.com
Website: www.allencarr.com

Cambridge

Tel: 020 8944 7761
Therapists: Emma Hudson, Sam Bonner
Email: mail@allencarr.com
Website: www.allencarr.com

Cardiff

Tel: +44 (0)117 950 1441
Therapist: David Key
Email: stop@easywaysouthwest.com
Website: www.allencarr.com

Colchester

Tel: 01621 819812
Therapist: Lynton Humphries
Email: contact@easywaylynton.com
Website: www.allencarr.com

Coventry

Tel: 0800 321 3007
Therapist: Rob Fielding
Email: info@easywaycoventry.co.uk
Website: www.allencarr.com

Crewe

Tel: +44 (0)1270 664176
Therapist: Debbie Brewer-West
Email: debbie@easyway2stopsmoking.co.uk
Website: www.allencarr.com

Cumbria

Tel: 0800 077 6187
Therapist: Mark Keen
Email: mark@easywaycumbria.co.uk
Website: www.allencarr.com

Derby

Tel: +44 (0)1270 664176
Therapists: Debbie Brewer-West
Email: debbie@easyway2stopsmoking.co.uk
Website: www.allencarr.com

Exeter

Tel: +44 (0)117 950 1441
Therapist: David Key
Email: stop@easywaysouthwest.com
Website: www.allencarr.com

Guernsey

Tel: 0800 077 6187
Therapist: Mark Keen
Email: mark@easywaylancashire.co.uk
Website: www.allencarr.com

Ipswich

Tel: 01621 819812
Therapist: Lynton Humphries
Email: contact@easywaylynton.com
Website: www.allencarr.com

Isle of Man

Tel: 0800 077 6187
Therapist: Mark Keen
Email: mark@easywaylancashire.co.uk
Website: www.allencarr.com

Jersey

Tel: 0800 077 6187
Therapist: Mark Keen
Email: mark@easywaylancashire.co.uk

Website: www.allencarr.com

Kent
Tel: 0800 028 7257
Therapists: John Dicey, Colleen Dwyer, Emma Hudson, Sam Carroll
Email: info@allencarr.com
Website: www.allencarr.com

Lancashire
Tel: 0800 077 6187
Therapist: Mark Keen
Email: mark@easywaylancashire.co.uk
Website: www.allencarr.com

Leeds
Tel: 0800 077 6187
Therapist: Mark Keen
Email: mark@easywaylancashire.co.uk
Website: www.allencarr.com

Leicester
Tel: 0800 321 3007
Therapist: Rob Fielding
Email: info@easywayleicester.co.uk
Website: www.allencarr.com

Lincoln
Tel: 0800 321 3007
Therapist: Rob Fielding
Email: info@easywayleicester.co.uk
Website: www.allencarr.com

Liverpool
Tel: 0800 077 6187
Therapist: Mark Keen
Email: mark@easywayliverpool.co.uk
Website: www.allencarr.com

Manchester
Tel: 0800 077 6187
Therapist: Mark Keen
Email: mark@easywaylancashire.co.uk
Website: www.allencarr.com

Manchester – alcohol sessions
Tel: 07936 712942
Therapist: Mike Connolly
Email: info@stopdrinkingnorth.co.uk
Website: www.allencarr.com

Milton Keynes
Tel: 020 8944 7761
Therapists: Emma Hudson, Sam Bonner
Email: mail@allencarr.com
Website: www.allencarr.com

Newcastle/North East
Tel: 0800 077 6187
Therapist: Mark Keen
Email: info@easywaynortheast.co.uk
Website: www.allencarr.com

Nottingham
Tel: +44 (0)1270 664176
Therapist: Debbie Brewer-West
Email: debbie@easyway2stopsmoking.co.uk
Website: www.allencarr.com

Oxford
Tel: 020 8944 7761
Therapists: Emma Hudson, Sam Bonner
Email: mail@allencarr.com
Website: www.allencarr.com

Reading
Tel: 0800 028 7257
Therapists: John Dicey, Colleen Dwyer, Emma Hudson, Sam Carroll
Email: info@allencarr.com
Website: www.allencarr.com

SCOTLAND
Glasgow and Edinburgh
Tel: +44 (0)131 449 7858
Therapists: Paul Melvin and Jim McCreadie
Email: info@easywayscotland.co.uk
Website: www.allencarr.com

Sheffield
Tel: 01924 830768
Therapist: Joseph Spencer
Email: joseph@easywaysheffield.co.uk
Website: www.allencarr.com

Shrewsbury
Tel: +44 (0)1270 664176
Therapist: Debbie Brewer-West
Email: debbie@easyway2stopsmoking.co.uk
Website: www.allencarr.com

Southampton
Tel: 0800 028 7257
Therapists: John Dicey, Colleen Dwyer, Emma Hudson, Sam Carroll
Email: info@allencarr.com
Website: www.allencarr.com

Southport
Tel: 0800 077 6187
Therapist: Mark Keen
Email: mark@easywaylancashire.co.uk
Website: www.allencarr.com

Staines/Heathrow
Tel: 0800 028 7257
Therapists: John Dicey, Colleen Dwyer, Emma Hudson, Sam Carroll
Email: info@allencarr.com
Website: www.allencarr.com

Stevenage
Tel: 020 8944 7761
Therapists: Emma Hudson, Sam Bonner
Email: mail@allencarr.com
Website: www.allencarr.com

Stoke
Tel: +44 (0)1270 664176
Therapist: Debbie Brewer-West
Email: debbie@
easyway2stopsmoking.co.uk
Website: www.allencarr.com

Surrey
Park House, 14 Pepys Road, Raynes Park,
London SW20 8NH
Tel: +44 (0)20 8944 7761
Fax: +44 (0)20 8944 8619
Therapists: John Dicey, Colleen Dwyer, Crispin
Hay, Emma Hudson, Rob Fielding, Sam Carroll
Email: mail@allencarr.com
Website: www.allencarr.com

Swindon
Tel: +44 (0)117 950 1441
Therapist: David Key
Email: stopsmoking@easywaybristol.co.uk
Website: www.allencarr.com

Telford
Tel: +44 (0)1270 664176
Therapist: Debbie Brewer-West
Email: debbie@easyway2stopsmoking.co.uk
Website: www.allencarr.com

Watford
Tel: 020 8944 7761
Therapists: Emma Hudson, Sam Bonner
Email: mail@allencarr.com
Website: www.allencarr.com

WORLDWIDE CLINICS

REPUBLIC OF IRELAND
Dublin and Cork
Lo-Call (From ROI) 1 890 ESYWAY (37 99 29)
Tel: +353 (0)1 499 9010 (4 lines)
Therapists: Brenda Sweeney and Team
Email: info@allencarr.ie
Website: www.allencarr.com

AUSTRALIA

Queensland
Tel: 1300 848 028
Therapist: Natalie Clays
Email: natalie@allencarr.com.auu
Website: www.allencarr.com

Northern Territory – Darwin
Tel: 1300 55 78 01
Therapist: Dianne Fisher and Natalie Clays
Email: wa@allencarr.com.au
Website: www.allencarr.com

New South Wales, Sydney, A.C.T.
Tel & Fax: 1300 848 028
Therapist: Natalie Clays
Email: natalie@allencarr.com.au
Website: www.allencarr.com

South Australia – Adelaide
Tel: 1300 848 028
Therapist: Jaime Reed
Email: sa@allencarr.au
Website: www.allencarr.com

Victoria
Tel: +61 (0)3 9894 8866 or 1300 790 565
Therapist: Gail Morris
Email: vic@allencarr.com.au
Website: www.allencarr.com

Western Australia – Perth
Tel: 1300 55 78 01
Therapist: Dianne Fisher
Email: wa@allencarr.com.au
Website: www.allencarr.com

AUSTRIA
Sessions held throughout Austria
Freephone: 0800RAUCHEN (0800 7282436)
Tel: +43 (0)3512 44755
Therapists: Erich Kellermann and Team
Email: info@allen-carr.at
Website: www.allencarr.com

BELGIUM
Antwerp
Tel: +32 (0)3 281 6255
Fax: +32 (0)3 744 0608
Therapist: Dirk Nielandt
Email: info@allencarr.be
Website: www.allencarr.com

BRAZIL
Sau Paulo
Therapists: Alberto Steinberg & Lilian Brunstein
Email: contato@easywaysp.com.br
Tel Lilian - (55) (11) 99456-0153
Tel Alberto - (55) (11) 99325-6514
Website: www.allencarr.com

BULGARIA
Tel: 0800 14104 / +359 899 88 99 07
Therapist: Rumyana Kostadinova
Email: rk@nepushaveche.com
Website: www.allencarr.com

CANADA
Toll free: +1-866 666 4299 / +1 905 849 7736
English Therapist: Damian O'Hara
French Therapist: Rejean Belanger
Regular seminars held in Toronto, Vancouver and
Montreal
Corporate programs available throughout
Canada
Email: info@theeasywaytostopsmoking.com
Website: www.allencarr.com

CHILE
Tel: +56 2 4744587
Therapist: Claudia Sarmiento
Email: contacto@allencarr.cl

Website: www.allencarr.com

COLOMBIA – Bogota
Therapist: – Felipe Sanint Echeverri
Tel: +57 3158681043
E-mail: info@nomascigarillos.com
Website: www.allencarr.com

CZECH REPUBLIC – opening 2015
Website: www.allencarr.com

DENMARK
Sessions held throughout Denmark
Tel: +45 70267711
Therapist: Mette Fonss
Email: mette@easyway.dk
Website: www.allencarr.com

ECUADOR
Tel & Fax: +593 (0)2 2820 920
Therapist: Ingrid Wittich
Email: toisan@pi.pro.ec
Website: www.allencarr.com

ESTONIA
Tel: +372 733 0044
Therapist: Henry Jakobson
Email: info@allencarr.ee
Website: www.allencarr.com

FINLAND
Tel: +358-(0)45 3544099
Therapist: Janne Ström
Email: info@allencarr.fi
Website: www.allencarr.com

FRANCE
Sessions held throughout France
Freephone: 0800 FUMEUR
Tel: +33 (4) 91 33 54 55
Therapists: Erick Serre and Team
Email: info@allencarr.fr
Website: www.allencarr.com

GERMANY
Sessions held throughout Germany
Freephone: 08000RAUCHEN (0800 07282436)
Tel: +49 (0) 8031 90190-0
Therapists: Erich Kellermann and Team
Email: info@allen-carr.de
Website: www.allencarr.com

GREECE
Sessions held throughout Greece
Tel: +30 210 5224087
Therapist: Panos Tzouras
Email: panos@allencarr.gr
Website: www.allencarr.com

GUATEMALA
Tel: +502 2362 0000
Therapist: Michelle Binford
Email: bienvenid@dejedefumarfacil.com
Website: www.allencarr.com

HONG KONG
Email: info@easywayhongkong.com
Website: www.allencarr.com

HUNGARY
Seminars in Budapest and 12 other cities across Hungary
Tel: 06 80 624 426 (freephone) or +36 20 580 9244
Therapist: Gabor Szasz and Gyorgy Domjan
Email: szasz.gabor@allencarr.hu
Website: www.allencarr.com

ICELAND
Reykjavik
Tel: +354 588 7060
Therapist: Petur Einarsson
Email: easyway@easyway.is
Website: www.allencarr.com

INDIA
Bangalore & Chennai
Tel: +91 (0)80 41603838
Therapist: Suresh Shottam
Email: info@easywaytostopsmoking.co.in
Website: www.allencarr.com

ISRAEL
Sessions held throughout Israel
Tel: +972 (0)3 6212525
Therapists: Ramy Romanovsky, Orit Rozen, Kinneret Triffon
Email: info@allencarr.co.il
Website: www.allencarr.com

ITALY
Sessions held throughout Italy
Tel/Fax: +39 (0)2 7060 2438
Therapists: Francesca Cesati and Team
Email: info@easywayitalia.com
Website: www.allencarr.com

JAPAN
Sessions held throughout Japan
www.allencarr.com

LEBANON
Tel/Fax: +961 1 791 5565
Mob: +961 76 789555
Therapist: Sadek El-Assaad
Email: stopsmoking@allencarr.com.lb
Website: www.allencarr.com

LITHUANIA
Tel: +370 694 29591
Therapist: Evaldas Zvirblis
Email: info@mestirukyti.eu
Website: www.allencarr.com

MAURITIUS
Tel: +230 5727 5103
Therapist: Heidi Hoareau
Email: info@allencarr.mu
Website: www.allencarr.com

MEXICO
Sessions held throughout Mexico
Tel: +52 55 2623 0631
Therapists: Jorge Davo and Mario Campuzano
Otero
Email: info@allencarr-mexico.com
Website: www.allencarr.com

NETHERLANDS
Sessions held throughout the Netherlands
Allen Carr's Easyway 'stoppen met roken'
Tel: (+31)53 478 43 62 /(+31)900 786 77 37
Email: info@allencarr.nl
Website: www.allencarr.com

NEW ZEALAND
North Island – Auckland
Tel: +64 (0)9 817 5396
Therapist: Vickie Macrae
Email: vickie@easywaynz.co.nz
Website: www.allencarr.com

South Island – Christchurch
Tel: 0800 327992
Therapist: Laurence Cooke
Email: laurence@easywaysouthisland.co.nz
Website: www.allencarr.com

NORWAY
Oslo
Tel: +47 93 20 09 11
Therapist: René Adde
Email: post@easyway-norge.no
Website: www.allencarr.com

PERU
Lima
Tel: +511 637 7310
Therapist: Luis Loranca
Email: lloranca@dejardefumaraltoque.com
Website: www.allencarr.com

POLAND
Sessions held throughout Poland
Tel: +48 (0)22 621 36 11
Therapist: Anna Kabat
Email: info@allen-carr.pl
Website: www.allencarr.com

PORTUGAL
Oporto
Tel: +351 22 9958698
Therapist: Ria Slof
Email: info@comodeixardefumar.com
Website: www.allencarr.com

ROMANIA
Tel: +40 (0) 7321 3 8383
Therapist: Diana Vasiliu
Email: raspunsuri@allencarr.ro
Website: www.allencarr.com

RUSSIA
Moscow
Tel: +7 495 644 64 26
Therapist: Alexander Formin
Email: info@allencarr.ru
Website: www.allencarr.com
Crimea, Simferopol
Tel: +38 095 781 8180
Therapist: Yuriy Zhvakolyuk
Email: zhvakolyuk@gmail.com
Website: www.allencarr.com

St Petersburg – opening 2015
Website: www.allencarr.com

SERBIA
Belgrade
Tel: +381 (0)11 308 8686
Email: office@allencarr.co.rs
Website: www.allencarr.com

SINGAPORE
Tel: +65 6329 9660
Therapist: Pam Oei
Email: pam@allencarr.com.sg
Website: www.allencarr.com

SLOVAKIA – opening 2015
Website: www.allencarr.com

SLOVENIA
Tel: 00386 (0) 40 77 61 77
Therapist: Gregor Server
Email: easyway@easyway.si
Website: www.allencarr.com

SOUTH AFRICA
Sessions held throughout South Africa
National Booking Line: 0861 100 200
Head Office: 15 Draper Square, Draper St,
Claremont 7708, Cape Town
Cape Town: Dr Charles Nel
Tel: +27 (0)21 851 5883
Mobile: 083 600 5555
Therapists: Dr Charles Nel, Malcolm Robinson
and Team
Email: easyway@allencarr.co.za
Website: www.allencarr.com

SOUTH KOREA
Seoul
Tel: +82 (0)70 4227 1862
Therapist: Yousung Cha
Email: yscha08@gmail.com
Website: www.allencarr.com

SPAIN
Madrid
Tel: +34 91 6296030
Therapist: Lola Camacho
Email: info@dejardefumar.org
Website: www.allencarr.com

SWEDEN
Tel: +46 70 695 6850
Therpaists: Nina Ljungqvist, Renée Johansson
Email: info@easyway.nu
Website: www.allencarr.com

SWITZERLAND
Sessions held throughout Switzerland
Freephone: 0800RAUCHEN
(0800/728 2436)
Tel: +41 (0)52 383 3773
Fax: +41 (0)52 3833774
Therapists: Cyrill Argast and Team
For sessions in Suisse Romand and Svizzera Italiana:
Tel: 0800 386 387
Email: info@allen-carr.ch
Website: www.allencarr.com

TURKEY
Sessions held throughout Turkey
Tel: +90 212 358 5307
Therapist: Emre Ustunucar
Email: info@allencarrturkiye.com
Website: www.allencarr.com

UKRAINE
Kiev
Tel: +38 044 353 2934
Therapist: Kirill Stekhin
Email: kirill@allencarr.kiev.ua
Website: www.allencarr.com

USA
Central information and bookings:
Toll free: 1 866 666 4299 / New York: 212- 330 9194
Email: info@theeasywaytostopsmoking.com
Website: www.allencarr.com
Seminars held regularly in New York, Los Angeles, Denver and Houston
Corporate programs available throughout the USA
Mailing address: 1133 Broadway, Suite 706, New York, NY 10010
Therapists: Damian O'Hara, Collene Curran, David Skeist

OTHER ALLEN CARR PUBLICATIONS

Allen Carr's revolutionary Easyway method is available in a wide variety of formats, including digitally as audiobooks and ebooks, and has been successfully applied to a broad range of subjects.
For more information about Easyway publications, please visit www.easywaypublishing.com

Stop Smoking Now (with hypnotherapy CD)
ISBN: 978-1-84837-373-0

Stop Smoking with Allen Carr (with 70-minute audio CD)
ISBN: 978-1-84858-997-1

Easyway Express: Stop Smoking and Quit E-cigarettes
Ebook

The Illustrated Easy Way to Stop Smoking
ISBN: 978-1-84837-930-5

Finally Free!
ISBN: 978-1-84858-979-7

The Easy Way for Women to Stop Smoking
ISBN: 978-1-84837-464-5

The Illustrated Easy Way for Women to Stop Smoking
ISBN: 978-1-78212-495-5

How to Be a Happy Non-Smoker
Ebook

Smoking Sucks (Parent Guide with 16-page comic)
ISBN: 978-0-572-03320-0

No More Ashtrays
ISBN: 978-1-84858-083-1

The Little Book of Quitting
ISBN: 978-1-45490-242-3

The Only Way to Stop Smoking Permanently
ISBN: 978-0-14-024475-1

The Easy Way to Stop Smoking
ISBN: 978-0-71819-455-0

How to Stop Your Child Smoking
ISBN: 978-0-14027-836-1

Stop Drinking Now (with hypnotherapy CD)
ISBN: 978-1-84837-982-4

The Illustrated Easy Way to Stop Drinking
ISBN: 978-1-78404-504-3

The Easy Way to Control Alcohol
ISBN: 978-1-84837-465-2

No More Hangovers
ISBN: 978-1-84837-555-0

Lose Weight Now (with hypnotherapy CD)
ISBN: 978-1-84837-720-2

No More Diets
ISBN: 978-1-84837-554-3

The Easyweigh to Lose Weight
ISBN: 978-0-14026-358-9

The Easy Way to Stop Gambling
ISBN: 978-1-78212-448-1

No More Gambling
Ebook

No More Worrying
ISBN: 978-1-84837-826-1

Allen Carr's Get Out of Debt Now
ISBN: 978-1-84837-98-7

No More Debt
Ebook

No More Fear of Flying
ISBN: 978-1-78404-279-0

The Easy Way to Enjoy Flying
ISBN: 978-0-71819-458-3

Burning Ambition
ISBN: 978-0-14103-030-2

The Nicotine Conspiracy
Ebook

Packing It In The Easy Way (the autobiography)
ISBN: 978-0-14101-517-0

Want Easyway on your smartphone or tablet?

Search for "Allen Carr" in your app store.

Easyway publications are also available as audiobooks.

Visit www.easywaypublishing.com to find out more.

DISCOUNT VOUCHER
for
ALLEN CARR'S
EASYWAY CLINICS

Recover the price of this book when you attend an
Allen Carr's Easyway Clinic
anywhere in the world!

Allen Carr's Easyway has a global network of stop
smoking clinics where we guarantee you'll find it easy
to stop smoking or your money back.

**The success rate based on this
unique money-back guarantee is over 90%.**

Sessions addressing weight, alcohol and other
drug addictions are also available at certain clinics.

When you book your session, mention this
voucher and you'll receive a discount of
the price of this book. Contact your nearest
clinic for more information on how the sessions
work and to book your appointment.

**Details of Allen Carr's Easyway
Clinics can be found at**
www.allencarr.com
or call 0800 389 2115

This offer is not valid in conjunction with any other offer/promotion.